Climbing Out of Depression

Climbing Out of Depression

A Practical Guide to Real and Immediate Help

Sue Atkinson

JEREMY P. TARCHER/PENGUIN

a member of Penguin Group (USA) Inc.

New York

JEREMY P. TARCHER/PENGUIN
Published by the Penguin Group
Penguin Group (USA) Inc., 375 Hudson Street, New York, New York 10014, USA • Penguin Group (Canada),
90 Eglinton Avenue East, Suite 700, Toronto, Ontario M4P 2Y3, Canada (a division of Pearson Canada Inc.) •
Penguin Books Ltd, 80 Strand, London WC2R 0RL, England • Penguin Ireland, 25 St Stephen's Green,
Dublin 2, Ireland (a division of Penguin Books Ltd) • Penguin Group (Australia), 250 Camberwell Road,
Camberwell, Victoria 3124, Australia (a division of Pearson Australia Group Pty Ltd) • Penguin Books
India Pvt Ltd, 11 Community Centre, Panchsheel Park, New Delhi–110 017, India • Penguin Group (NZ),
67 Apollo Drive, Rosedale, North Shore 0632, New Zealand (a division of Pearson New Zealand Ltd) •
Penguin Books (South Africa) (Pty) Ltd, 24 Sturdee Avenue, Rosebank, Johannesburg 2196, South Africa

Penguin Books Ltd, Registered Offices: 80 Strand, London WC2R 0RL, England

Most Tarcher/Penguin books are available at special quantity discounts for bulk purchase for sales, promotions,
premiums, fund-raising, and educational needs. Special books or book excerpts also can be created to fit specific
needs. For details, write Penguin Group (USA) Inc. Special Markets, 375 Hudson Street, New York, NY 10014.

ISBN 978-1-58542-685-0

Printed in the United States of America
1   3   5   7   9   10   8   6   4   2

Neither the publisher nor the author is engaged in rendering professional advice or services to the individual
reader. The ideas, procedures, and suggestions contained in this book are not intended as a substitute for
consulting with your physician. All matters regarding your health require medical supervision. Neither the author
nor the publisher shall be liable or responsible for any loss or damage allegedly arising from any information or
suggestion in this book.

While the author has made every effort to provide accurate telephone numbers and Internet addresses at the time
of publication, neither the publisher nor the author assumes any responsibility for errors, or for changes that
occur after publication. Further, the publisher does not have any control over and does not assume any
responsibility for author or third-party websites or their content.

For those who held on to the lifeline
when the going was tough,
for those who sat with me at the bottom of the cliff
and held my hand,
and for those who showed me,
by their love,
that the climb was worthwhile

Contents

Preface to the new edition

It has been so thrilling to meet and talk to depressed people and their caregivers since *Climbing Out of Depression* was first published twelve years ago. People from all over the world have written to me, and I've made some good friends through those letters. I have asked some of these people to make suggestions as to how the book could be improved.

I've tried to incorporate a number of those suggestions into this new edition, but some information is better found elsewhere. For example, I didn't think I should focus on medication. Such information gets out of date, and it is best to talk to a doctor or look at the Depression Alliance website.

What has changed?

I have seen such dramatic change in some depressed people (including myself), and that is something for all of us to hold on to.

We can and do change!

Some people I have met resist that change with great energy and vigor. Others have steadily improved to the point where they can completely turn their lives around.

Some go back to work.

Some make much better relationships.

Some start up a new self-help group for other depressed people.

Some say how much they enjoy being fit enough to laugh and play with their children or go out with their friends.

What's new in this edition?

In this second edition of the book, I have made some changes to the text, either where I felt it important to add to my new understanding of depression or where I have changed my mind!

Now that I run workshops (as a sufferer, not a trained professional) with depressed people, caregivers, and counselors, I've learned much from brave and struggling people, and from those who care for them. Thank you so much to those people who have helped me make this new edition clearer and more up-to-date.

I've added much more about coping strategies to manage our depression better. This was one of the most requested topics at sessions I've run for self-help groups, and I have started working on these strategies also with groups of counselors.

There is more about forgiveness because this is something so many of us need to keep working at.

There is some more about our caregivers, the dear people who try so hard to care. What an undervalued group they are—some of them just children—who give their all, trying to make life a bit better for us.

I've updated the resources at the back of the book, including references to the web, where we all can get up-to-date information but where we can also get misled, so do take care. Definitely don't buy medication on the web.

Stages of depression?

Some people are convinced that there are stages to depression. At one very obvious level, there are three stages.

- *Being so utterly depressed that normal life is impossible. (This is when we need to rest and hide.)*
- *Getting a bit better. (This is when we sometimes need to rest but at other times we must* do something!*)*
- *Feeling much better—cheerful, positive, and able to get on with life—and having the determination to learn from what we have been through.*

People who have massive "highs" and devastating "lows" might want to say they have two very clear stages and seem to veer between them, sometimes within days, much to the confusion of those around them.

- *Very "high" while planning far too much (without being even vaguely realistic) or spending too much money or being massively creative: composing a symphony or hatching some completely new scheme.*
- *So depressed that death seems quite inviting.*

And without much in between!

The problem with stages

The problem I see in putting too much emphasis on stages is that it is so common to think we have slumped down to the very depths of depression again when actually we may find that it was just a blip and we are really still on the way up, not back at the bottom of the cliff.

So we need to be careful. If we insist we are at the bottom of the cliff, we might be quite wrong and be limiting our recovery. It is all too easy to get so stuck in our depression that we start to lose hope and we may develop the habit of being "center stage" at home with everyone running around us! We insist that we are still unable to *do anything*. This is very dangerous thinking!

Being creative

Of course, depression has many causes, but over the years, watching friends, family, and acquaintances going in and out of depressed phases, I see creativity in their lives as one of the most significant aspects of their climb up from depression.

If we don't use our creative self, we are in danger of stagnating. We can become restless, fed up, edgy, irritable, and unhappy. Maybe for some people that is the beginning of their depression.

This creativity can be there in the most ordinary of things:

- preparing food
- sharing and listening in a self-help group
- taking pleasure from reading a good novel and talking to a friend about it
- our own thoughts and day dreams after listening to the radio

All of these things get our right-brain creativity out there and exercised, instead of being trapped and ignored because of our complaining or our preoccupations with earning money or keeping our house so clean and tidy that our neighbors will admire us or whatever else we do to cramp our creative life.

Get a hold of the facts

Depressed people often ask me if they are going mad, a question that worried me for years. Depression feels like madness but it isn't. Depression is a recognizable medical condition. It is not something that we have invented to shirk our responsibilities! It is *not* something to feel guilty about.

The chemical factor

In chapter 6, I write about how some depression is due to our body chemistry being out of balance. Knowing this can be a great relief to a sufferer because it can lessen the sense of it being "all my fault." But some psychologists insist that depression is all about getting our head straight, and thus we don't need antidepressants. This view has tended to make me feel a bit feeble and guilty, but last week I went through a rather dramatic example demonstrating how important the chemical factor can be.

I had to take two courses of antibiotics to get over a horrid urinary infection, and I became utterly depressed. I found it hard to get out of bed, I was weepy, and I felt so bad that I could hardly believe I could change so drastically in a few days.

Many pots of yogurt and a few days later I was better, so I'm in total agreement with those doctors who say that we need to acknowledge that some depression is an illness (rather like having thyroid problems or diabetes) caused by a chemical imbalance in the body.

Remember that the next time you are told to "pull yourself together" and "get over it." There is no need for the huge amount of guilt that we tend to feel, and our mood will change when the body chemistry is back to where it should be.

Do something

More and more, I have come to see that the key to getting better from depression is to *do something,* even if it is only one small thing, such as recycling junk mail as soon as it comes through the mailbox, rather than finding the kitchen table so full of papers there is no space to eat.

The most important thing I have done to help myself get better is to write in my journal. I've been encouraged by learning that some psychologists see the start of change as:

• monitoring *what is going on (as we jot down things we are thinking and feeling)*

- *starting to* analyze and see patterns *in what we write (such as "I always panic when that relative phones me")*
- *seeing for ourselves through this process how we might change our lives for the better and* doing something to make that change happen

Again, the things we change can be tiny things.

One thing at a time

It's hopeless to think that we can change our lives quickly and easily. We need lots of time. I found that I was trying to change too much and too quickly, so I now just focus on one thing at a time. I write this thing on my "word wall."

I got so anxious about things that I realized my quality of life was poor. I wanted to be able to be more at peace. So *peace* is on my "word wall." I look at it. I think about it. I try to work toward feeling more peaceful by relaxing, and so on.

The principle here is to choose one thing at a time and work on that until you can see some change—or until something more important comes to mind.

A friend gave me a beautiful tiny notebook, and now I keep a copy of my word-wall words in that. I take the tiny notebook with me when I take a trip or a vacation, when I have plenty of time to think and might be able to add related words to other bricks or to start a new page with a new key word.

Too introspective?

When I'm leading workshops for depressed people, I talk about keeping a journal. Often someone says, "Isn't that too introspective?"

Well, only in the sense that anything you do to try to make your depression better might be seen as introspective: talking to your doctor, taking a five-minute break at work, telling a friend honestly how you feel, or deciding to eat healthier. You could do any of these things to nurture yourself, journalling being just one of the ways to do that creatively.

As I write, I find out what I am thinking. I learn more about myself. Writing is one way to help us reflect on our depressed feelings in order to recognize patterns in what we do and think. This is crucial if we are to overcome our depressed feelings and behavior. (If you really hate writing, try just one word at a time on a "word wall," as above.)

Journalling can be hugely powerful in our climb out of depression!

Necessary work

Almost all depression seems to be about some kind of loss, and in chapter 6, I've added a bit more about the loss of our comfortable ways of seeing the world and the changes we make to our beliefs as we grow older—the necessary work of depression.

Finding treasure?

One of the most thrilling things I have found from talking to people once they have recovered from depression is that some will say they have found some kind of "treasure" through it. This does not mean that they are glad they were depressed but that they have discovered something they would have missed had they not been depressed.

Some talk of:

- repairing relationships
- learning the true value of friendship
- getting a more realistic view of what life is about
- learning to put the important things in life first

That last point comes up over and over again. When people become very stressed, maybe at work, maybe trying to get rich, maybe trying to get "to the top," and so on, a bout of severe depression teaches them that it isn't money or status or power that makes them happy.

Happiness comes more through:

- living at peace
- making plenty of family time
- loving others
- giving our time and energy to help the human race and to help keep our planet from burning up

and so on.

I do hope you find this book useful and healing.

Sue Atkinson
Norwich, England, 2005

Climbing Out of Depression

Introduction

How to use this book

- The book is written to be read in little bits. The attention span of most people who are depressed is so limited that reading in small chunks is often all that is possible.
- Dip into the parts of the book that appeal to you today or that most fit your mood.
- Skip what doesn't seem relevant to you today.
- Go back later to the parts that you don't understand or that make you angry.
- Each chapter is more or less self-contained, but I have sometimes referred to other relevant bits on the same theme at the end of the chapters. In this way you can use the book to follow up certain points that may seem particularly relevant to you.
- Try the activities. Don't just read them! The book is intended to spark your own thinking.
- Ideas for other reading are given at the end (pages 187–188), along with the addresses of some useful organizations.
- Using the book with a friend may help you to get more from it.

Part 1
Rock Climbing for Lemmings

1

Instant cures?

This book is intended for people who feel
  sad
  lonely
  despairing
  depressed
  suicidal

It does not contain any miracle cure, instant healing, or health, wealth, and happiness just over the page. Any book that offers such things, or any person who tells you a simple way to feel better ("Count your blessings, dear," or "Eat more fresh fruit and vegetables") is to be regarded with the very deepest suspicion.

What this book isn't

This book isn't *10 Easy Steps out of Depression*. I have a horror of those books! They may work well for some people, but what if I take the steps and I'm just as depressed at the end of it all? I just know that would happen to me.

In my experiences of depression over several years, recovery is never simple and certainly never easy. Those people who tell us that it is easy and that we must pull our socks up are simply wrong!

This book is less of a "how-to," and much more of a "why," book. I think if we know why, we will be in a better position to take appropriate steps to know how to get out of it all.

It does have some "how to" suggestions, but they are only that, suggestions based on things that I have done or that others I know have done. Some of the activities have been suggested by people who work with those who are depressed.

My qualifications for writing the book

I have been depressed many times in my life, and I have talked with and lived alongside other depressed people during those years. And I survived!

I'm not writing it as an expert, nor am I writing it because I think I have found all the answers. It is a book about seeking out the right questions. Not everything in the book will help you. You may hate bits of it. Ignore these and go on to another section, but when you feel stronger, return to the bit you hated and ask yourself why you hated it. What was it that got to you?

The reality of depression

It is a very, very difficult thing to climb up out of depression. One day we seem to be near the top. The next we realize that we are actually down near the bottom again.

But we can do it! That is one of the Great Truths about depression: It doesn't last forever.

For each of us the climb is slightly different. What works for me or for my friend may not work for you. Or it may not work for you just yet. But as with any tool or aid for life's problems, what we get out of it is directly proportional to what we put in. You need to *do* the activities to get the most from the book.

**I hear and I forget,
I see and I remember,
I do and I understand.**
—*Old Chinese proverb*

On days when depression is very bad, it may be best just to browse through some of the book, and return to the activities another day.

Getting better from depression is not a spectator sport

Getting better from depression is like rock climbing: No one ever completed a climb by just thinking about it. We only get up with a great deal of blood, sweat, and tears; a fair bit of courage; some falling off and starting again; and a large amount of determination.

Before you give up and decide that you have none of those qualities, it is important to see that even opening this book took some courage. For the depressed person, doing *anything* takes courage.

There will be no major solution to the suffering of humanity until we reach some understanding of who we are, what the purpose of creation was, what happens after death. Until those questions are resolved we are caught.
—*Woody Allen*

I suggest that you need a notebook. It doesn't have to be a smart, thick, hardbacked journal. It can be a cheap little spiral-bound from the market. What is important is that it is something you feel happy with. It is yours and only yours. No one else reads it. So you need to find a place to keep it safe.

- Maybe writing fills you with horror! Don't worry. Write if it is helpful. If it isn't, just ignore those activities that are about writing.
- This "journal," as I will call it, can be as important as you want it to be.
- If you are more of a talker than a writer, you might just want to jot down notes of what you want to discuss with someone.
- The important thing is that we externalize our ideas somehow.

For me it is writing. For some people it is talking, or painting, or cooking, or engaging in an aggressive sport. If we do use a journal or notebook, one of its important functions is to help to get our thoughts and feelings outside of us. There are other ways that we can choose to externalize our feeling and thinking, such as

talking
cooking
gardening
drawing
painting
dancing

By putting our feelings and thoughts outside ourselves in these ways, we can get clues as to what makes us depressed. For example, if, as we dig in the garden, we are thinking repeatedly about how to get along with some member of our family, it is highly likely there is a problem that is getting us down far more than we may have realized.

If we try to get our thinking out where we can look at it, we will have some power over it. If we have some power over what we are thinking, it will not control us so much. We will be more in charge of our lives. This power over the direction of our lives is important in our recovery from depression.

My own journals over the years contain ideas, thoughts, complaints, prayers, pencil sketches, and drafts of furious letters to people. When I was in mental hospitals it also contained a calendar; I had become so confused I couldn't work out even which season it was. Your journal may be very different, and the suggested activities are just starting points. They are not a set of fixed things you must do.

I lay in bed staring at the darkness, hopeless. For weeks I had been unable to eat or sleep and was gripped with the fierceness of my neurosis. This time I knew I was not going to get better by myself.
—*Martha Maughon*

2

Why rock climbing?

The trouble with the rat race is that even if you win you're still a rat.
—*Lily Tomlin, actress*

One of my favorite activities is rock climbing. When I was sixteen I discovered that facing an almost impossible challenge energized me. I soon got hooked on the unbelievably fantastic feeling of getting to the top. Later on, after years of depression that lasted into my twenties and thirties, I took up climbing again. I began to see it as a metaphor for life: It feels like hell while you are doing it, but once you reach the top you feel that nothing will ever be so difficult again. So I'm using rock climbing as an illustration of the struggle out of depression.

Why lemmings?

I identify with lemmings, little brown furry creatures of the Scandinavian tundra known for leaping off cliffs to commit suicide. When naturalists tell us that this is not what they really do, we feel a bit cheated!

Apparently what lemmings really do is emigrate. In some years—known as "lemming years"—there are too many of them and food is scarce. No one is really quite sure what causes one of these "lemming years," but litter after litter of baby lemmings is born. Perhaps the weather is good or food is plentiful, but, whatever it is, lemmings go on and on having babies. Maybe Mrs. Lemming just feels broody. It could be a result of changes in the climate or in their food sources. As yet, naturalists are not sure.

This overpopulation activates their instinct to spread out on the overcrowded slopes of the hillside. As if their lives depended on it, hundreds of lemmings scurry off in a great swathe or whatever the collective noun for lemmings is—a "courage" of lemmings maybe—and if they happen to get to the cliff edge, over they go.

It is this fatal quirk that has led to the belief that they commit suicide. What they are really doing is rushing off to find some island or patch of hillside where they can feed in peace without having friends and relations gobbled up by bands of marauding goshawks. So it is all really done for the survival of the species, but given the height of some Norwegian fjord cliffs, it is hardly surprising that many of them perish in pursuit of their survival. Hence their acts of courage have been mistaken by humans as suicide.

Lemmings have been suspected of suicide for so long that it is hard to change the image. That goes for a lot of us. How we *were* is what we get stuck with.

Depressed people can identify with lemmings. We feel the urge to emigrate, that is, to get away from all that haunts us, or wish that we could start life all over again. For many of us, life is so terrible that we believe that death would be a sort of relief. Certainly it could be no worse than the present.

So this book is written for:

- those who want to jump, or have jumped, "over the cliff" (some may feel they were pushed)
- those sitting at the foot of the cliff
- those who are so overwhelmed and confused that they have no idea of where they are and how they got there and certainly no idea of what they might do about it—or even if they want to do anything about it because it is all so awful
- those who, looking up at the cliff, really want to be back at the top again but feel they will need a lot of help if they are ever going to attempt the climb

We promise according to our hopes and perform according to our fears.
—*François Duc de La Rochefoucauld*

Part 2
How Did
I Get Here?

3

Sitting on the rocks
at the foot of the cliff

**Depression is as universal as the common cold.
It can be so slight as to be hardly worth the
name ... or at the other extreme, it can almost
totally paralyze action.**
—*Myra Chave-Jones*

One of the very worst things in deepest depression and despair is the
utter loneliness. That devastating feeling of total alienation from every
other living thing in the universe. The intense mental pain and anxiety
of isolation separates depression and despair from the much less
painful experiences of helplessness and sadness that all of us suffer
from time to time. But the dividing line is thin.

Some depressed people are able to carry on with a relatively normal
life. For others, certain stages of depression are too dark and too empty
for them to do anything at all. Some people can manage a few things
for survival, such as eating and drinking; some have ceased to be able
to do even that.

> **None of us can help the things life has done to us.
> They're done before you realize it, and once they're done
> they make you do other things until at last everything
> comes between you and what you'd like to be, and you
> have lost your true self forever.**
> —*Eugene O'Neill*

Depression is such a devastating experience that we ask ourselves
very basic questions about life, death, and human experience. If there
is a God, he seems to be some angry monster, some cruel alien who is
laughing at us from his comfortable seat on high. So maybe we don't

want him as our God anyway; he has deserted us, just when we needed him most.

I've tried appeasing this God: "If you will just . . ." "If you will take these feelings away, I'll love you forever and do anything you want." But it hasn't worked. I know I don't deserve to be loved. It's all my fault. I feel guilty. Ashamed. Hopeless. Useless. Stupid. A fraud.

People are laughing at me, and I feel so afraid. I know I'm no good. In the depths of the night, fear grips my heart. It paralyzes my mind. But most of all, I feel very, very alone.

We're all in this together—by ourselves.
—*Lily Tomlin*

It is the dark abyss of depression. The pit. The bell jar. Hell. The foot of the steepest cliff at midnight. The tide is coming in and there is no escape.

How do I know if I am depressed?

It is possible that you don't know you are depressed. The ordinary sadness that we come to expect—often referred to as "the blues"—is very difficult to distinguish from mild depression. If we are experiencing depression for the first time we may simply not know what is happening to us. People talk about depression a little more nowadays than they used to, but it is still an area of mystery. This makes it very hard for us to cope. We feel "odd," out of step with others, and rather mystified about what is going on. Much of this book is about why we are depressed. It is much easier to get out of depression if we understand it and see what it is all about.

The symptoms of depression

At first it may be no more than an insidious creeping sadness and lethargy. In mild depression that may be all we experience. But there are many different levels of depression, from this vague feeling of malaise to extreme symptoms such as hearing voices, hallucinations, and the suicidal feelings that sometimes accompany the deepest depressions. The other symptoms are many and varied and include:

irritability
withdrawal
crying
anger
weight loss or gain
lack of concentration
violent mood swings
fear and anxiety
hypersensitivity to criticism
guilt
hopelessness
tearfulness
feelings of inadequacy and worthlessness
changed sleep pattern—either wakefulness or
an inability to get to sleep
no interest in food or overeating as a kind of
comfort
uncontrollable feelings of total despair

There seems no point in doing anything, and the things that used to motivate us, like cooking, or gardening, a favorite hobby, going to the cinema, sex, music, or whatever, now fail to interest us. It is this change of lifestyle that is often the clearest indicator of depression. You may have few other symptoms, but inside yourself you know that something is wrong. That is depression.

What does it feel like?

At its worst, depression is like a thick cloud that descends on us totally unexpectedly. It is fear of the deepest darkness. It is like walking alone on the Yorkshire Moors at night. Like living on an alien planet. Like suddenly and unexpectedly becoming blind, deaf, dumb, paralyzed, and penniless. But, because you are none of these things, the world expects you to cope.

But you can't. And no one can hear your cry. You can speak, but the world has no way to hear you. You are utterly terrified. You want to evaporate. You want out of life.

The mass of men lead lives of quiet desperation.
—Henry Thoreau

A broken leg tells the world there is something wrong, but when your mind shuts off from reality in order to survive, you have no easy way to tell the world that you are hurting inside.

Images of depression

Feelings of darkness and of being imprisoned give rise to various pictures of depression. I've always thought of it as a very deep, narrow, straight-sided pit, or the foot of a very steep cliff. It is totally dark and there are no footholds. Scrabbling up the edge is hopeless. I am alone, and it is breathtakingly silent.

Others who are depressed see it as a prison, a steep hill, a cage dangling over a bottomless pit. Whatever the image, the feelings have similar characteristics. But this is not much comfort. To every depressed person, the feelings of being cut off from other human beings are stark and painful.

Why didn't anyone tell me that life could be like this?

You do not have to be very depressed to realize that there are only a perceptive few who see your pain, but they may well not know what to do or say. The others, sadly often your closest relatives, friends, sometimes even your doctor, will insist that you get a grip on yourself, "snap out of it," and get on with living.

It is then that your world takes on the ghastly reality of the isolation of the depressed. You know that no other human being could have felt like this because someone would have told you, warned you that it could be this bad. But the experience cannot be put into words or communicated. You are right that no one else ever felt like this because each depression is unique. It takes on a life of its own. Its root causes are specific to you.

And nothing to look backward to with pride
And nothing to look forward to with hope.
—Robert Frost

You ask for help, and they stuff you with pills. They won't listen because you need a million hours. You need a million hugs. You need a million words of reassurance. These you cannot have, for the world is busy with its own life and priorities. The reality is that you are what the world might call "mentally ill," and that hurts. It hurts like hell.

People who say there are simple answers are wrong, and their cliché-ridden talk drives you further into depression.

Now I am setting out into the unknown. It will take me a long while to work through the grief. There are no shortcuts; it has to be gone through.
—*Madeleine L'Engle*

4

Finding the cave:
ideas for the very bad days

We only think when we are confronted with a problem.
—*John Dewey*

From where you are there may seem to be no footholds, no roots to hold on to, no one to hand you a rope. It's pitch dark. The rock is jagged. It is slippery with seaweed. Every time you make a move you get wet feet. You are tired. Hungry. Cold. Utterly miserable and incapable of even looking at the cliff, never mind attempting to climb it.

Part of you doesn't care about the fact that any moment now the tide will wash you away, but some little inner spark prompts you to remember that before the sun set, you saw a cave just over to the left. If you went now, maybe you would make it. It isn't far. At least it would be warmer.

I have called the first step out of depression "finding the cave." It's not the top of the hill—it's a long way from where we want to end up—

but it will keep us from being washed away by the tide. This is what I mean:

1 Do something!

You're reading this book, so that will do for a start. Don't aim too high. Make a cup of coffee, or switch on the radio.

On better days it may be appropriate to ask yourself why you feel this bad today. What are you actually feeling? But I don't do that on the worst days. I just try to exist for the next ten minutes, then the next . . .

2 Find your "cave"; at least it will be warm and dry.

My "cave" is my bed. I get under the quilt with my cuddly toy and refuse to come out for hours (it used to be days) on end. For some people the "cave" is watching the television, reading, cooking, or walking. It doesn't matter where we escape to. It is important that we escape from the pressures of our world and do something that pleases us enough to stop the crying and the spiraling down into total oblivion.

For me, part of the "escape" is absorbing myself in stories, either my own or those of others. I get into the world of the story and leave the other world behind for a bit. I feel safe in my own world. Once I feel safe I can think of coming out of my "cave."

It is vital to recognize at this stage that if crawling under the quilt is all you can manage to do, *don't feel guilty about it! That will only make you feel worse.*

Anyone near you, your family for example, may well need training in recognizing that retreating to your cave is all you are capable of. They won't necessarily understand. They will almost certainly be irritated at your apparent self-centeredness.

Yes, everything they say just makes it worse. That's how it is with depression. It is such a shock to every human being who experiences it exactly because it is almost impossible to communicate the overwhelmingly dreadful feeling to anyone else. Each depressed person wonders why he or she is going through something that is so devastatingly painful that the thought of death is almost a comfort.

So find your "cave." Get into it, and stay there. Your family will *not* starve without you there for a while. The company will *not* grind to a halt. The world will *not* come to an end because you retreat to your bed. You are *not* actually indispensable, and at the moment you may have to allow yourself to be a little bit self-protective. A basic rule for a depressed person is "be kind to yourself."

3   *Realize that these very worst moments do actually pass.*
If you can recognize at all that now is a little better than, say, four o'clock this morning, a crucial skill in surviving human existence is within your grasp. *Everything in the world as we know it comes to an end.* Good things. Bad things. They all end. These feelings will, one day, not be there. But today they are there and they hurt.

If we are going to think positively about climbing the cliff, it helps to know what's going on in our minds and our emotions when we are at the bottom. Somehow we need to understand what our pain is trying to tell us. What is it that is underneath our depression?

- It is a surprisingly common human experience to be at the foot of the cliff in utter depression (one in five people—a rather scary statistic).
- It is not your "fault" or anything to feel guilty about.
- It is not something you can just "snap out of"—despite what people say!

My life as an actor has been a form of therapy. . . . [It has allowed me] to free myself of some unutterable burden.
—*Sir Anthony Hopkins*

In the next chapters we will look at **what depression is** and **some of the possible causes** of depression.

5

What is depression?

Depression is the worst nonphysical pain known to humans.
—*A doctor*

One of the most striking things about depression is its horrifying inevitability. Quite frankly, I just don't believe those who say they have never had a day of depression in their lives! I think it more likely either that they deny the strength of their feelings—perhaps because they cannot cope with them—or that they are just not able to recognize the symptoms!

There are different levels of depression. Many people who are depressed get better on their own, but feeling low can escalate, and some of us are all too familiar with the confusion and hopelessness that can characterize a deeper depression. Doctors regard this as an illness and sometimes may treat it with drugs, electroconvulsive therapy (ECT), or with a talking treatment—therapy or counseling.

Some of us experience depression so severely that our lives are changed significantly as we struggle to find some meaning and purpose. When the depression lifts, we know that we will never be the same person again. It will always leave a scar. Paradoxically, though, it may be that we will be left more "whole" than we were before, more of a "complete" human being.

Severe depression is being recognized as one of the major health concerns of this century.
—*Dr. Richard Winter*

I'm told that depression affects almost every culture throughout the world. Some people think that there is more of it in sophisticated cultures, and that seems to make a lot of sense. We know, though, that it is not just modern life that provokes depression. The Greek physician Hippocrates described it four hundred years before Jesus lived.

The list of famous depressives is very reassuring! It includes Beethoven, Schumann, William Cowper, Isaac Newton, Franz Kafka, Darwin, Tolstoy, and Winston Churchill (who called it his "black dog").

For some, one particular form of depressive illness can have some advantages. It is what doctors call manic or bipolar depression, which is characterized by extreme mood swings. As well as times of deepest melancholy there are also times of elation. On a "high," the person can be so creative and engage in such intense activity that his or her level of achievement is outstanding. I'm told that many inventors did their best work in these manic phases. It is not surprising, therefore, that it is sometimes said that genius is close to mental illness.

The other side of the story, though, is that often during such a "high" the afflicted person will undertake a totally unrealistic project that cannot be completed. There isn't the cash to pay for it. There isn't the expertise to execute the plans. This results in further depression.

Many writers, artists, and particularly poets are likely to experience depression. I find this very comforting, and it certainly rings true to my experience: Many of the depressed people I meet tend to be very sensitive and creative, and something I enjoy exploring with artists of all kinds is that interesting link between depression and creativity.

Different kinds of depression

There is a set of labels for depressed people who go to the doctor's office. For example, a person who has symptoms of depression, such as sleeplessness and a loss of interest in anything but who otherwise seems to have no problems, might be given the label "endogenous depression." A person whose depression is mostly a response to very difficult circumstances, such as bereavement, might be said to have "reactive depression."

The umbrella term for the different kinds of serious depression that doctors seem to use is "clinical depression." (So reactive and endogenous depression, if they are serious enough, are said to be clinical depression.) It seems that some doctors say to people, "You are depressed but not clinically depressed." The outcome of this can be that the patient gets no medication or any other help or advice.

Of course people get better without taking medication. In the natural ups and downs of life, our mood changes. But if you feel your depression is more than just feeling a bit sad, and you were given no support, go back to the doctor and talk this through.

Some doctors seem to love labels! One problem I have noticed, though, is that if people were to go to a different doctor, they might get a different label! If they were to go to someone not trained in medicine but in psychology, or in therapy, they might not get a label at all (or any medication).

We need to be cautious about labels; there are quite a lot of them. Here are some:

> *endogenous depression*
> *reactive depression*
> *manic depression (a bipolar disorder)*
> *cyclic depression*
> *postnatal depression*
> *anxiety state*

There are many more. They are probably Deeply Meaningful, but they may well not tell the whole truth. As doctors change and develop their understanding of depression, so these labels change, and there is up-to-date information on the web or in Dr. Virginia Edwards's book *Depression and Bipolar Disorders: Everything You Need to Know* (see Resources at the back).

Endogenous depression

This label means that the depression is thought of as coming from within the person, and for many doctors it indicates some kind of imbalance in the body chemistry. For others, such as psychotherapists, however, if there is no obvious reason for depression it might signal that there are causes that are still covered up. These may be from childhood, from bereavement, or from some other unresolved trauma.

Some therapists use "talking therapy" to approach this kind of depression. Some doctors might correct the imbalance in the body with some kind of medication. Some of us benefit from both therapy and medication.

My personal belief is that those who think that endogenous depression has no cause other than body chemistry are not usually seeing the whole story. It may be a depression where the story has yet to be told. I lived with the label for years. It made me feel so helpless that I descended into total passivity: "There is nothing I can do about this. I'm ill." Then I had some help from a psychologist who said, "Tell me your story." That was the beginning of my climb up out of depression.

Reactive depression

Depression is very often a reaction to events or circumstances. If important things happen to us, we react. The death of someone we love, or the thought of leaving our home, or the news that we or a friend has cancer can cause us to plummet into despair.

Some of that despair can be the result of trying to contain our unrecognized rage. How could that so-called God of love let such a lovely person get cancer? The despair can also be rooted in fear:

People the same age as me are dying.
I won't know anyone in the new town.
When my children leave home I will feel all alone.

All of these situations can cause depression. We can't cope with them so we retreat into reactive depression instead.

Children who have suffered sustained periods of pain repress trauma in order to survive. This repressed emotion sows the seed from which later depression might bloom.

Antidepressant medication

Whatever kind of depression you have, it is important to see your doctor. He or she may well offer some medication; I have found it a lifesaver.

There are several different types of antidepressant drugs, and it is often a case of finding the one that will suit you the best. They take several days to take effect, so swapping from one to another may mean an agonizingly long time before the tablets can work, but it may be worth persevering. Although I don't think drugs are the complete answer, they can lift a person's mood enough so that he or she can cope better with life and work at the real causes. I still take tablets. Check the web for information on antidepressants.

A "person," not a "case"

What gave me my first insight into the idea that doctors and psychiatrists might not always be right with their labels was that each practitioner I saw gave me a different one. I've received most of those listed above! Not only was that incredibly funny, it also was utterly disconcerting. I didn't see myself as a "cyclic depressive with paranoid tendencies." I was a hurting person, and I wanted to know why. I thought if I understood my hurt I could get better and go back home and look after my babies.

Labels and treatment with pills, injections, and electrodes seemed not to address me as a human being. I never found pills or electrodes particularly therapeutic. They controlled me. They made me passive. They stopped me from expressing my stress. Gradually, with medication and ECT, I would feel better (which was wonderful), and then I would be allowed home. Then if things got bad again, the process would start all over again.

I don't mean that psychiatrists, or doctors, or drugs are no help to anyone; on the contrary, it is very important to be in touch with your doctor if your depression is serious. What I do mean is that for some depressed people the labels and the treatments that some doctors tend to give are not always relevant.

It was important that I be allowed to exist beyond the "box" that some doctors wanted to put me in. (Woe betide me if I behaved in a way that my label didn't account for!) My climb up out of depression has been a gradual process involving millions of words and a lot of hugs. In fact, the only label I needed was "person."

**Answer me, O Lord, out of the goodness of your love;
in your great mercy turn to me.
Do not hide your face from your servant;
answer me quickly, for I am in trouble.**
—*The Psalmist*

6

What causes depression?

Most people get a fair amount of fun out of their lives, but on balance life is suffering, and only the very young or the very foolish imagine otherwise.
—*George Orwell*

The first and most important thing to say about the causes of depression is that there is no one simple answer. The causes can be complex and extremely difficult to unravel. Some people can say exactly why they are depressed, but others can't find an obvious reason. In some cases the reasons are a complex confusion of the past and present, and the twists and turns of the mind through a lifetime.

These complex factors can propel feelings of mild depression unnervingly and rapidly downward into a depression we may feel we never can escape from. This section outlines some of these possible factors.

Body chemistry out of balance?

There is a strong link between body chemistry and moods in both men and women. Many women recognize the raging tiger in themselves that emerges before their monthly period. Or, after childbirth, many women clutch their newborn babies knowing that they are "supposed" to be happy, but all they really want to do is weep. Their hormones are all over the place. A flu or other virus can also leave us feeling miserable. Other illnesses, especially long-term ones or those that take a lot out of us, can leave us depressed and unable to cope.

Depression, like the common cold, is no respecter of persons.
—*Myra Chave-Jones*

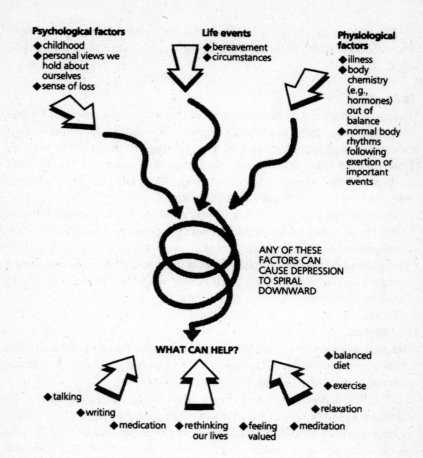

Psychological factors
- childhood
- personal views we hold about ourselves
- sense of loss

Life events
- bereavement
- circumstances

Physiological factors
- illness
- body chemistry (e.g., hormones) out of balance
- normal body rhythms following exertion or important events

ANY OF THESE FACTORS CAN CAUSE DEPRESSION TO SPIRAL DOWNWARD

WHAT CAN HELP?
- talking
- writing
- medication
- rethinking our lives
- feeling valued
- balanced diet
- exercise
- relaxation
- meditation

Taking antibiotics can sometimes cause depression. It may rob our bodies of things that are needed to keep us healthy (for example, we need microbes in our intestines in order to feel okay). There are chemicals in our food and drink, in the air, in the water, that can influence body function. Farmers feel ill after putting their sheep through certain sheep dips. Hay fever sufferers can feel wretched when pollen is in the atmosphere. Alcohol—not necessarily a lot of it—is a depressant. Some people have unrecognized food allergies that can cause them to feel low.

These are the sorts of triggers that can lead to longer and more intense depression, especially if other life circumstances are less than ideal.

Burnout

When my children became teenagers, they became moody and low following any really big event. The crucial exams or the important concert seemed inevitably to lead to a feeling of flatness: "Why ever did I put all that effort in? It wasn't that important, and now I don't want to do anything except sit here and mope." Maybe these are the times when our body is asking for rest after stress.

Burnout can happen to anyone who puts heart and soul into things. It is often seen as something that happens to those who work desperately hard over a long period of time, such as the young father who pushes himself at work and then goes home to the stresses of a family. The depression that often comes with that is perhaps a very "healthy" reaction.

Childhood

Reactive depression often comes from responses made in childhood. As little children we were unable to understand the world, and we inevitably got our climbing ropes all confused.

Childhood doesn't have to have been particularly traumatic for someone to carry scars into adult life. Often, quite unintentionally, a parent can give a child the message that she is not valued just for who she is. Love becomes conditional: "If you are a good boy like Tom next door . . . "; "We love you when . . ."; "You have to get straight A's for us to really love you and approve of you."

It is not necessarily the apparently important things that affect a child; he may misinterpret the seemingly insignificant: "Daddy doesn't love me because he said he would read me a story, but then the phone rang and he went downstairs." If he feels of less value than a phone call, he will easily come to believe that he is of little value.

It's always winter and never Christmas.
—*Mr. Tumnus* in *C. S. Lewis's* The Lion, the Witch and the Wardrobe

Depression and lifestyle

Some people's circumstances are problematic and depressing. Sometimes, in some extraordinary way, we repeat difficult experiences from our childhood in adult life. It is said, for example, that we tend to parent our children in the way that we were parented. (Of course, that is not always true.)

Sometimes it seems that we *need* to keep hold of childhood problems. For example, the daughter of an abusive alcoholic may marry a man similarly afflicted, and so re-create the dynamic. People can get trapped in ongoing patterns of behavior.

Depression and personality

There may be things in an individual's life that are difficult or impossible to change, and this affects them severely. I think if I lived in a famine-stricken country I would be pretty depressed! It can also be that someone's personality tends toward the gloomy. Take Puddleglum, for example, in *The Silver Chair* by C. S. Lewis, or Eeyore—quite the gloomiest character in children's fiction—who lived in the Hundred Acre Wood with Christopher Robin. There would be absolutely no point in telling either of them to cheer up. It just isn't in their nature to be like that!

Some people are like that too. It doesn't mean, though, that we need to spend our whole lives in total misery. It just might be that for some of us, life will always seem problematic and gloomy. (But take care; too much contact with someone who constantly focuses on the negative can be disastrous if we are depressed or have a tendency to become depressed.)

Passing on depression?

Is depression hereditary? Can I pass it on to my child? It would seem that any child who grows up with at least one depressed parent might well develop a depressing view of life. But it can develop in many ways: being bullied at school year after year, feeling unloved and rejected by a parent. Many things are able to make a child become depressed. It is hard to know if it is "nature" (they were born that way) or "nurture" (they become so because of circumstances).

In a seminar I led recently, a young woman asked if she was

harming her children because she was depressed. She felt that she was a terrible mother. She thought that she was ruining their childhood and that they would become depressed like her.

My heart went out to her. I didn't want to reply in public; I wanted to hug her. What I struggled to say was that despite having me for a mother, often depressed and crying, my own children are two of the most wonderful, mature, and balanced people you could meet. They tell me I am a wonderful mother. We are such good friends.

So I tried to reassure this young woman that she is almost certainly a "good-enough" mother. (See chapter 9.) Children are quite resilient. They survive. We do not need to feel guilty that we are not perfect parents! Children survive somehow, so if our kids need therapy at some time in their lives, that's how it is.

But of course, we must push ourselves to do things when we would rather crawl under the duvet. We push ourselves because we love our children. As in any aspect of our life, putting other people's needs before our own brings us long-term contentment and happiness. But we must plan "time out."

In spite of depression, we can raise happy and healthy children.

Depression and loss

To lose an object of significance is a depressing event. If our house is repossessed because we can't keep up the payments, or if we lose a precious possession, we are naturally upset. Losing a person through death or desertion or some other kind of separation is often very much harder to deal with than the loss of a material object.

There are other kinds of loss, though, that are even more difficult to get a grip on. Much of my own depression was due to a loss of self-esteem. I thought I was of no value. If I feel I have no value, then I have no place in the world. If I don't think I belong, I will feel insecure. It is impossible to function successfully in the world with these kinds of losses dominating our thoughts.

Depression and "necessary work"

Everyone in the universe faces difficulties at some times in his or her life, and as we struggle along we often have to give up our familiar ways of doing things, our beliefs about the world and the people in it, and grow and adapt. So as we grow older, our thinking matures as we learn from life, with all its joys and disasters. Some people call this the "necessary work" that comes with depression. We all have to work at life, but if we get stuck or cannot bear to lose our comfortable ways of thinking and behaving, we mourn this loss of the familiar in our depression.

If we can rethink, change, adapt, and embrace our new maturity, letting go of the familiar, we will be fine. If we dig our heels in and refuse to change, or if we are too frightened to change, or if something obstructs this necessary change, we plunge down the cliff into depression.

So some people see depression as an inevitable part of life, and it is this idea that leads some people to say that as they do the "necessary work" they find treasures in depression. Yes, there is loss, but the gains can be greater in the long term.

But let's be quite clear that it doesn't help us while we're in the depths of depression to be told that we will find a treasure within it. There must be easier and less-gut-wrenching ways to find good things in our life.

Depression and guilt

For me, guilt is one of the hardest things to face in depression. When I talk to others who are depressed, guilt invariably shows up on the agenda. I can see that much of their guilt is unnecessary, that they are just being hypersensitive. When it comes to my own guilt, I "know" that it is real!

Guilt is very complex. It's not at all easy to see where it comes from. Of course, some guilt is real, and necessary. If we really have hurt someone, for example, we may still feel guilty even after we've apologized. If we deal with it by pushing it deep down inside ourselves, danger lies ahead.

There is something about perfectionism that induces guilt. I know women who feel guilty if they don't clear the table and wash up right after a meal, or if there is a speck of dust in the house, or if the meal is not ready when the family wants it. People who come to my house can see that I am far from a perfectionist in that sense. But it is important to recognize that there is a kind of perfectionism that can really get to us and go unrecognized for what it is. We sometimes—maybe even unknowingly—set ourselves impossible standards. Sometimes we feel guilty when we are not really guilty.

Depression and anger

Depression can be seen as the reverse side of anger. Myra Chave-Jones describes it as "frozen rage" in her book *Coping with Depression*. That makes a lot of sense to me and to every single depressed person I have talked to in any depth. We do not feel safe enough to express our anger, so we suppress it. Our bodies try to contain that internalized anger, but they fail, and depression (or an ulcer or a heart attack) is the result.

Depression and the stresses of life

Going through a divorce, moving a household, having problems at work or with kids is enough to make anyone feel that life is too much. The key to recovering from depression that is related to stress is to recognize that stress level and then plan a phase of recovery. (We will work at planning for recovery later on.) However, the laws of the universe being what they are, this will be the year Grandma dies, our neighbor gets cancer, and a new five-lane highway is built at the end of our garden.

Depression and anxiety

For many people, anxiety is very closely linked with depression. I've talked to lots of people about this, and many of us seem to really struggle to keep overwhelming anxiety from ruining our lives.

One man told me recently that he spoils most of his time off from work by worrying the whole weekend that something he said to a colleague on Friday will mean that there will be terrible trouble on Monday morning or that he will lose his job or the friendship forever. As we talked about this, people around us were nodding, saying they were like that too.

The ways in which I manage my anxiety are mentioned throughout this book, things like relaxation and meditation, along with the coping strategies for depression described in chapters 12 and 13.

Depression and women

More women than men get depressed. There could be many reasons for this, such as hormone imbalances, pregnancy, and so on. But a woman gets it wrong whatever she does. If she stays at home to look after her baby, she is boring. If she goes to work and parks the children out at the local day care, she is a terrible mother. Even if no one actually says that, that's what we tell ourselves! Guilt from being unable to do it right as a mother, lover, friend, colleague, and person comes to the surface easily.

If we try to break out of the mold that society makes for women, then our troubles really start. I don't have any answers to this, but it is interesting that women sometimes seem to be the dumping ground for so many of the ills of society. Those problems not caused by mothers are caused by teachers, so as a teacher and a mother I get it both ways!

I read in a newspaper about some research where it was found that if women go to a doctor with a symptom such as a pounding heart, it is likely they will be given tranquilizers and antidepressants. However, if men complain of identical symptoms, they will be more likely to be referred to a heart specialist. I suppose men are meant to be tough and macho and not get depressed or anxious. I think that must be incredibly hard to deal with for a man who is depressed.

Depression is complicated

Depression leaves precious little in reserve to face the daily knocks of life. It is the anniversary of a death, it's raining, you still feel a bit wobbly from a tummy bug. Burning the toast is then a major disaster, and you spiral downward.

Things that haven't bothered us until now come to the surface and hurt. The depression following redundancy is not necessarily just about that rejection. Similar pain in childhood may surface and need to be worked through.

Maybe the only thing that we can say with certainty about depression is that it is mindbogglingly complicated!

The causes of depression are complex, and an important part of our climb up is to try to understand the reasons why we are sitting at the foot of the cliff. We need to "hear" what our body is trying to tell us and uncover buried memories. Sorting out those reasons is not easy. It's not comfortable, and it can't be done overnight. But this book is about giving it a try.

Activity

Here are some first steps:

- Draw a diagram like the one in chapter 6. Try to put on some of the things that have caused you to lose your grip on life.
- Start to tell your own story. You could do this by making an overall sketch of critical events. What were the really important moments for you?

A journey of a thousand miles begins with a single step.

For more on **negative thinking** see chapter 19; **losses**, chapter 27; **anger**, chapter 23; **guilt**, chapter 24; **stress**, chapter 28; the **"good-enough" principle**, chapter 9.

7

Being kind to ourselves

It may be that those who do most, dream most.
—*Stephen Leacock*

When you are depressed it is hard to be kind to yourself. You tend to run yourself down, to focus on negative characteristics ("I'm no good at . . ."), and to feel in some spectacularly odd way that this depression is deserved.

We need to learn to be kind to ourselves both at the foot of the cliff and as we undertake the climb up. How do we learn to be kind to ourselves?

- With difficulty! Especially if we believe that somehow we deserve this "punishment." That it's evidence that God is fed up with us and has chosen to strike us with a thunderbolt of depression.
- Be realistic. People don't recover from depression in a day by pushing themselves beyond what they are able to do, or by sitting around moaning, or by telling themselves that things must be perfect. Doing so tends to cause us to slither down the cliff even further.
- Accept what is happening. Persistently refusing to believe we are actually depressed, or feeling guilty that it is happening, or not acknowledging how much it hurts will only delay the climb up the cliff face.
- Be patient. We don't usually get to the top of the climb just by wanting to be there. Wanting is a great start, but the actual climb takes time and effort. It is like dieting. *Patience* is a key word. Lose weight fast, and it will come back on the minute you dive for the chocolate. Just as "healthy eating" for the rest of our life is better than dieting, so the best plan for dealing with depression is the long-term plan. We can work at this with a caregiver if we have one; we can both eat healthily.
- Get plenty of rest. Many of us experience overwhelming fatigue when we are depressed. This gets very mixed up with feelings that it isn't worth doing anything anyway. So we may not always appreciate that this fatigue may well be a complex mixture of despair, exhausting anxiety, and stress. We need plenty of sleep, but sleep is sometimes difficult in depression. Taking tablets to help you sleep is okay for the really bad times.
- Get plenty of exercise. Surprisingly, although we often feel exhausted by being awake for ten minutes, getting some exercise can make us feel less tired. It relieves stress too. But go gently.
- Do things you enjoy. It isn't selfish to take ourselves out for the day to go bird watching or to the cinema. It is all part of our survival strategy, and everyone needs one.
- Take a break from caring for the baby if you have postpartum depression. Teaming up with another mother may help. You can take turns caring for your babies to have some child-free time. The baby will be fine. We are better mothers if we take a break.

Blessed are you who weep now, for you will laugh.
—*Jesus, in the Gospel of Matthew*

Activity

What can I do to be kind to myself today?

- List the things you like doing. Put the list up where you will see it. Add to it when you think of other good things.
- Make time to do some of those things!

This section was all about the reasons why we might be sitting at the foot of the cliff in depression. In the next section I discuss the issues involved in **climbing up** out of it.

Part 3
Is Climbing for Me?

8

Someone to talk to

I'm a spiritual person and prayer is useful.
—*Madonna*

If we are going to think about climbing up out of depression, there will be many questions that need answering. Climbing out of depression is as difficult and demanding as climbing up a cliff face.

- Am I sure that it will be worth the effort?
- What will it be like?

If we decide to climb up, there are several things that we need. First we're going to need someone to talk to. Actually finding this person, someone who really understands, is incredibly reassuring. Maybe that is why "talking therapies" seem to work so well in helping people out of depression. Developing a deep relationship with someone is healing: There is someone there. I'm not totally alone. Someone values me.

When we reveal our confused muddle of hopelessness and despair, the greatest gift we can be given is gentle and sensitive handling of these doubts and fears. When someone takes our ramblings and responds with tenderness, we feel understood. The world seems a less frightening place. They don't have to speak because we do not always need words to comfort us. It is more the look in their eyes, that acceptance of us as a person, where we are. It makes the dreadful searing pain that we try so desperately, and always inadequately, to express seem shared and therefore a little more bearable.

For a few moments the pain and the dreadful loneliness recede. We feel a tug on the lifeline. It makes a silent impact on our body. We have connected with a human being. Something in our inner world feels strengthened. A basic human need is satisfied, albeit briefly.

Although we can do some bits of the climb on our own, it is much better if we have someone to talk to.

Too many cooks . . . ?

But this sharing can also lead us into places of the greatest danger. Knowing that we need this human compassion and sharing, we can open ourselves up unwisely. Sometimes we talk to too many people. Maybe it is the belief that if we share something with enough people, one of them will understand.

Trying to talk to and rely on lots of people is dangerous, a case of "too many lifeline holders spoil the climb." Our indecision as to who will hold the lifeline could leave people unsure of whether they should be bracing themselves for a fall.

If we talk to too many people it can also make us rather superficial. Trying to express our fears and loneliness to just one trusted friend will help us delve deeper into the problem. Expressing it to six means we stay superficial. That's probably why we do it.

Trusting

To find a special friend is a gift, but it is not a gift that is easy to receive. It is very difficult to accept it, and it involves great trust. However, if we are going to climb successfully we do need to find someone we can trust.

If we attempt the climb relying on one person's grip on the lifeline, he or she may well let us down. We know that. If we slip and put all our weight on it we are totally dependent on the strength of that person. We rely on that individual's ability to grip the rope as it runs through his or her fingers.

As we sit at the foot of the cliff contemplating the climb, we may not be able to take that risk. There may be no one, no human being who at that moment we feel we could trust with our lifeline.

There are lots of bits of the climb that come down to trusting. The leader's voice from below yells out that there is a handhold out of sight up to the left. When we try a tricky move we are trusting in the lifeline and in the strength of the person below holding on to the other end if we fall. We often follow instructions blindly, believing and trusting that the advice of our leader will be right. If we are going to climb, we need to think about whom we are going to trust.

Think

- Whom do I trust?
- Whom could I learn to trust?

To reveal myself openly and honestly takes the rawest kind of courage.
—*John Powell*

For information about **choosing a therapist** see chapter 11.

9

The "good enough" principle

Depression is without doubt the most unpleasant experience known to man.
—*A doctor*

Another thing that we will have to learn if we are going to climb is the "good enough" principle. (The phrase comes from the psychologist D. W. Winnicott.)

The idea of being "good enough" has helped me enormously over the years of depression, through motherhood, my professional life, and into midlife. What we have done—at work, at home, in the garden, or wherever—may not be fantastically wonderful, or perfect, or even the best that we could do, but is it good enough? Will it do? That is the real question.

Those of us who have a perfectionist streak, or who do not believe in ourselves very much, or who have so much to do that we just can't do things as well as we would like, can revolutionize our lives if we can grasp the "good enough" principle. If you

- constantly look at the dust and tell yourself how bad you are at housework
- look at the kids and think you should be taking them to the park and doing something "deeply meaningful" with them
- get a pie out of the oven and think how badly you have made it
- go into work on your day off
- always measure yourself by some external benchmark, such as trying to be as good a cook as your mother-in-law or as good at your job as the guy in the next office

you need to rethink things.

Is it good enough?
Asking yourself the question "Is it good enough?" is a great rescuer.

- I may not be a perfect parent, but the kids are happy, so maybe I'm good enough.
- I may not be doing this job as well as I could be if things were different, but it's good enough.
- I may not be the best cook in the world, but it's good enough to eat.
- I may not be putting up these shelves particularly well, but they will be straight enough.
- I may not be as good at this as Charlie, but I'm good enough.

Changing our standards
Trying to do things perfectly can sometimes mean that we do them less well. Can I learn to accept that doing it well enough is okay? Sometimes my standards (or other people's) are not realistic.

Why does it matter to me to be a fantastic mother/worker/boss/Christian/patient/partner/daughter/son?

I was trundling around with all my inadequacies and inner pain and loneliness and I yearned, desperately, to be something. I yearned to get out from where I was . . . some deep discontent within myself, actually some deep dislike of myself.
—*Sir Anthony Hopkins*

Activity

- Identify what seems not to be "good enough."
- Work on the idea of being "good enough."

10
Strategies for living

Pain is a teacher from whom we can learn much.
—*John Powell*

We need to learn some strategies for living. It's not just the bad days that need some kind of plan of action; we will climb better if we have some general strategies for every day.

I had no strategies for living before I was depressed. It was all a very hit-or-miss affair. As the bad times and crises came I was pushed around and tossed from one situation to the next. I never felt I had any control over my life. Whatever came at me hit me full in the face, and it seemed as if I could do nothing about it.

Now, I steer myself through the bad times much more. Instead of falling at the first sign of trouble, I find a place of refuge. As the debris falls off the cliff face, I seem to be able to duck.

Each crisis and down time (and there are plenty of them!) is now something of a challenge. With this sense of being more in control, I can almost watch myself handle it. That's a bit odd, but it gives me an enormous sense of achievement, even if my stomach does continue to lurch and my body cries out for Valium.

When disaster strikes now and I feel the panic rising, I know . . .

- I have been here so often before that I will get through it just like last time.
- My clinging-on skills get better every time.
- I now have a plan for the difficult times.

As I write this I know that my foothold feels extraordinarily insecure and shaky, and I sense that at any moment I may fall off. I look at all this positive stuff I'm writing, and it is very far from the way it actually feels at the moment. But somehow having survived as many crises as I have helps me believe that I may just have the strength to hold on. Each time I survive it seems to strengthen my grip on the cliff face.

Suffering can be used creatively.
—*Susan Howatch*

The trouble is that we cannot control some things. They hit us just because they are there. Today I learned of the death of a friend's twenty-five-year-old son. As I watch the news on the television, families weep for their loved ones.

When we hear these things, we are certain that we would never be able to cope if they happened to us. We hardly dare face our real emotions. If it were my child who had died, I feel that I would simply curl up and die myself.

Yet one of the strategies for living is not to live in the world of "what would happen if . . ." because gradually we learn that we somehow find the strength to face things. As a friend said to me about the death of her baby son, "You are given the strength when it happens, and then just enough for each day at a time."

"What if" and "if only"

"What if" and "if only" are phrases in the "self-talk" in our heads that we constantly need to watch out for. They are almost always negative ways of thinking. (More about **negative thinking** in chapter 19.)

We'll need a mask for survival

Every man has three characters—that which he exhibits, that which he has, and that which he thinks he has.
—*Alphonse Karr*

There is an image of a depressed person as someone who never smiles or who mopes about unable to do anything. For some that is how it is some of the time, but for others it is easy to laugh and to seem cheerful—and actually to be cheerful. Depressed people still have their sense of humor, and laughter is a good escape. And it can be an important part of our mask that we present to the world.

Developing a mask is not always a bad thing. It can be an important survival strategy. A mask has a good side and a bad side.

The good side of the mask

We learn that cheerful behavior somehow lifts our spirits. If we make the effort and actually manage to get ourselves out of the house in the morning and get on with our lives, we find to our astonishment that we can do it. It really isn't as bad as we thought it would be. (Usually!) The day as we imagine it at four in the morning does not seem as bad at four in the afternoon when we have done most of it. (Of course, there are some days that are so terrifyingly dreadful that we wish we had not made the effort.)

Someone once told me that you can become how you behave: "Happiness is a choice" and all that. At the time I thought that statement was simplistic. It would seem though that there is some truth in it.

The bad side of the mask

We can hide behind a mask and never face the truth of what we are really feeling. Many of us spend most of our lives doing that. We pretend that we are not frightened. We pretend that we are confident. We put on a brave face. We bury our emotions.

Buried emotions

We need to dig up our buried emotions. We have buried them alive, and they eventually struggle free. As these emotions emerge, we cannot recognize them for what they are. We have buried them for so long we have forgotten where they fit in. So the childhood emotion of the fear of being left alone breaks free at a time of crisis. But we don't express it as fear. Instead we become confused by our emotional state and perhaps lash out at someone we love. The fear has turned to aggression.

"Men don't cry," I hear a mother at school tell her five-year-old, who responds by hiding his real feelings. The hurt little boy retreats. It is never a surprise to me that the dear child who first came to school is quite a thug by the time he is nine. Those hurt and angry feelings are still inside him somewhere. Someone could have hugged them away when he was five, but no one did. Letting him scream and cry may have been a good thing because at least he would be expressing what he was really feeling *at the time he was feeling it.*

Now his feelings are all mixed up. His aggression seems to come from nowhere. It seems unrelated to whatever caused it.

A man cannot possibly be at peace with others until he has learned to be at peace with himself.
—*Bertrand Russell*

Most of us are aware of burying emotions. The "difficult" teenager may well be rebelling against something that happened when she was seven. An outburst of temper in the family today could be the result of something yesterday, or last year, that wasn't recognized as stressful at the time and so wasn't expressed.

Our depression is often about these buried feelings struggling to be acknowledged. If we are going to decide that "climbing is for me," we are going to have to work at coming to terms with them.

There are two kinds of pain that we forget. We forget hurts too trivial to bother about. We forget pains too horrible for our memory to manage.
—*Lewis Smedes*

Think

When we catch ourselves behaving unexpectedly we can get clues to our buried emotions.

- Why do I feel so tense at the thought of that particular person coming to visit?
- Why did I get so angry at such a trivial thing?
- Why did I get that panic attack just then?

Activity

There are all sorts of relaxation techniques on the market. It is a case of finding out which is best for you. I find the following sequence works well for me:

1. Doing some gentle exercise, if you feel up to it.
2. Listening to soothing music.
3. Taking a few slow, deep breaths.
4. Lying on the floor or the bed and tensing up every part of the body in turn. Start by tensing the feet and legs, hold for a few seconds, then let go. Then tense the muscles around the hips, hold, and let go. Gradually work each area of the body, not forgetting to include the neck and the face. On days when I have more time, I break the tensing down into smaller units—feet, calf muscles, knees, and so on—all separately.
5. End by tensing up every muscle you possibly can, hold, then let go.
6. Repeat sequence from step 3 if you are still finding it hard to relax.
7. When the muscles are relaxed, just lie quietly. Listen to the music and think of good things, for example watching the sun set over the sea. If you find worries creeping into your mind, try focusing on something positive and good: pictures, the music, or some progress you've made. Even on days when the worries don't go away, just a few minutes of "good-enough" relaxation is helpful.

Doing this relaxation routine regularly makes you better at it and it is easier to recognize the early signs of tension as they creep in physically.

• A long, soothing bath is good on days when the worries crowd in thick and fast. Some of the aromatherapy relaxing oils I've tried seem to help.

For relaxation during **panic attacks** see chapter 22.

11

What about professional therapy?

Every man passes his life in the search after friendship.
—Ralph Waldo Emerson

Not all of us have a friend who will listen in the way that we need. Sometimes, even if we are deeply loved and befriended, we still need someone else to talk to, someone who is outside of it all. Maybe this is the time to think about some professional counseling or therapy.

I know lots of people cannot afford therapy. But sometimes, if we have the energy to search, it's possible to find places that will adjust fees to what we can afford. Although therapy can be available through various organizations that receive subsidies, there are often very long waiting lists, and that can be agonizing.

The answer can be to find a group, either real or online, and start to share thoughts with others. I find "self-help" hugely healing. With no therapist around, in my experience, we can risk deeper relationships, and in so doing find that as we support others, we begin to feel better ourselves.

Now there is a lesson for life!

But therapy (or the usually more directive and low-key counseling) can be so healing. I am absolutely certain that the good quality of life I enjoy now is due to three remarkable therapists. They helped me to revolutionize my way of thinking about myself and others, to build up my self-esteem, and change my whole attitude toward life.

Choosing a therapist
There is plenty of information about different kinds of therapies. For example, the Depression Alliance publication *The Depression Handbook* is a quick guide (and one that will probably also be on the web soon); the book *Depression* by Dr. Virginia Edwards gives more detail.

If you are able to afford a private therapist, you might want to have "trial" sessions with a few before deciding on the best one for you. If someone in your self-help group can recommend one, that can be helpful. But beware: If both of you are seeing the same therapist, don't start comparing notes unless you are prepared for misunderstandings! What goes on in therapy is confidential, and the relationship that develops between you and the therapist is based on trust. I don't want to share my therapist with anyone. Irrational though it is, I don't even want to see the person that comes out of the therapist's room while I'm waiting to go in. You need to tread carefully.

My own rules are:

- If it is covered by health insurance, it is at least worth a go.
- If the therapist is apparently kind (as opposed to sitting behind a desk in a white coat telling you how stupid you are), then it is also worth exploring further.
- If what is on offer is only medication, you may need something else as well.
- If the therapist costs the earth but seems helpful, don't get hooked; he or she may want you to stick around for a bit to pay the mortgage. Proceed with caution.
- If you find a therapist you like, don't moan if she is an "interpersonal" therapist and you had set your heart on a "psychodynamic" therapist! If you get on with her, go with that! Some people search for months, even years, to find a therapist whom they trust enough to share their deepest fears. A good therapist will adjust her "methods" to fit your needs. She may use many types of therapy to deal with your problems. (I once experienced a totally "rigid" therapist—not a happy experience!)
- If money is short, adult education classes in addition to or instead of therapy can help. Classes in assertiveness or self-esteem have helped people I know to learn practical skills to manage their lives more creatively. Relaxation classes help to reduce stress. Learning a new skill can boost self-worth, and getting out of the house and *doing something* is the very thing that can help us up the climb.

Surviving therapy

I have a few survival pointers for therapy. Going into it is not an easy option. Some think that it should be on the life events list for high stress (see chapter 28). If it were, it would be pretty near the top! There is no doubt that therapy is tough, but if we can survive, it could be the most helpful thing that we could ever do to escape depression. (No promises, of course.)

Here are my rules for survival.

- It takes enormous courage, so tell the therapist if you are terrified.
- Expect it to get very much worse before it gets better.
- Even if after ten agonizing sessions you still think that the therapist hates your guts, it may be worth going on, but tell him or her.
- If the therapist is clearly an insensitive idiot, get out quickly.
- If the therapist tries to make connections between things that have been said, trying to get at what is underneath the words, and these connections make absolutely no sense whatsoever to you, it's important to say so. If the therapist's reaction is then to search further, or to try another approach, that's a good sign. If, on the other hand, the explanations sound like irrelevant garbage and you say so and you get put in your place and made to feel small, that may be a signal that the therapist needs therapy as much as you do! Rapid retreat could be called for if this persists, but it is crucial to explore it first with the therapist; it could well be a key issue.
- Don't just give up. Explore all problems thoroughly.
- It might be that, if things go badly, we have unrealistic expectations. Explore this with the therapist.
- If most of what is said is jargon, it is a good idea to say so. If the response is a real attempt at communication, go on. But if it is one that makes everything all your fault and "shows clearly that blah blah blah gobbledygook gobbledygook, don't you think so, Sue?" I don't know what to suggest. I never really figured that one out.
- All therapy is painful. It's not a good idea to give it up for that reason. However, it can be a good thing to stop if life gets so overwhelming that your survival is in doubt. There is a right time for things. We need to be ready to face things. There are also some therapeutic approaches that may not be right for you at that time. It's okay to say you can't cope with it right now.

There is a time for everything,
and a season for every activity under heaven:
a time to weep and a time to laugh,
a time to mourn and a time to dance,
a time to be silent and a time to speak.
—*Ecclesiastes*

12

Preparing for the bad days

**We thank thee that darkness reminds us
of light.**
—*T. S. Eliot*

If we are at all realistic about life, we soon come to see that some days are much worse than others. If we prepare for the bad days, we will be able to get through them much better, and the whole journey will seem a bit easier. Making the decision to try to climb up seems a more reasonable option.

Anyway, we have decided that we don't like our life as it is. In fact, it's awful! So we know we need to find ways to change it and get to the top of the cliff. When we get to a really difficult bit, we can think of this as an overhang. These are incredibly hard to deal with.

Our minds fill with thoughts that are unbearable. So this chapter and the next are about clarifying our survival strategies so that we can get through the very worst times.

Being prepared for terrible thoughts
There are two particular things that really shook me when I was trying to decide whether to take the risk of climbing out of depression.

The first was what someone said to me once when I was very depressed: *Depression is not the worst thing in the world.* I thought that very silly. Of course depression is the worst thing in the world. Everyone knows that. (All sensible people anyway.)

But it isn't. It is the things that are behind the depression that are much worse. I call these things the Deeply Meaningful Something-or-others (DMSs). Finding out what our own DMSs are is one of the crucial factors in the climb out of depression.

Much of this book is about finding out what those factors—the DMSs—behind depression are. Many people have particular ways of thinking or behaving that they developed in childhood and now have them trapped in guilt, fear, or anger. We have beliefs about ourselves and our circumstances that trap us in depression.

Many psychologists believe that we get depressed to escape from things that are too difficult for us to face.

I've had enough, Lord, take my life.
—*The prophet Elijah*

It's terrible to think that there is something worse than the living hell of depression. How can that possibly be? And if it is true, they— the Deeply Meaningful Something-or-others—must be horrendously terrible things if I escape from them into this!

The other really terrible thought is, as Dorothy Rowe puts it in her book *Depression: The Way Out of Your Prison*, that we hold the key with which we can let ourselves out of our prison of depression. When I first read that book, I thought it was so ridiculous that I didn't read any further than the first page. I was irritated and extremely cross that anyone should suggest that all I have to do is to get up and let myself out of this hellhole.

In my paranoid way I had turned it around and was saying "There you are: It's all your fault. All you have to do is get up and let yourself out. You are so pathetic."

Dorothy Rowe isn't saying it's all our "fault." I got it wrong. We do have the power (eventually) to get out (slowly and very painfully) of our depression, but it is not easy. It is not our "fault." We need courage and help to do it. We need comforters. We need a lot of time. We need to work hard at it.

Above all, we need to decide to set about changing our lives. An endless "tomorrow will do" will get us nowhere.

Learning to be prepared to change

It is difficult to contemplate change of any kind. To contemplate it while we are experiencing the pain of depression is almost impossible. But if we are to climb effectively then we need to change. Otherwise life could go on being this terrible, with depression lurking, ready to pounce on us at any moment.

The only sense that is common in the long run, is the sense of change—and we all instinctively avoid it.
—*E. B. White*

Most change happens very slowly. Sometimes it takes years of patience for some very small improvement. It may not be our unwillingness to change; it may be not knowing *how* to change. I would gladly exchange the hell of depression for "normal" life, but how?

How do we change?

The conditions that are conducive to change may well be different for every individual because depression is so very personal and varied. For me, much of the healing has come with time, as I have grown to understand why I was depressed in the first place and above all with having someone there beside me to help me.

When I became very depressed following the birth of my first longed-for baby, I was stuffed full of pills and talked at by psychiatrists, and so on. Some of that may well have been of some help. I don't know. What really resolved it was realizing what lay behind the depression. The crunch was that I was barely able to cope with my own rather fragile existence, trying as I was at that time to emerge from childhood and adolescent fears, fantasies, and traumas.

Now though, I was responsible for this child I had willingly created. This anxiety caused childhood traumas to creep out from the graves in which I had buried them. So my life was even more fragile because I was trying to climb up while holding on to this infant who leaked at both ends at all times of the day and night.

I was exhausted. I would sit and ask myself questions that worried me deeply. Will I be a terrible mother? How will I cope with the responsibility of him as well as me? Will he suffer in the way I did? It's all too terrible to face. So I won't face it. I'll pretend it isn't there: Depression!

Facing the Deeply Meaningful Something-or-others

We would willingly exchange our depression for any other kind of pain. (Medieval instruments of torture pale beside depression. Give me tearing out of the fingernails any day.) But unfortunately we are not seeing the situation as it really is. Unless our depression is caused solely by some chemical imbalance in our bodies, the causes of it are buried deep in the tangle of our lives: our living circumstances, our loves and our hates, our dreams and our fantasies, our childhood horrors, and the fears that lodge in the mind of any child, however well parented.

The right time

For some of us, it is simply not the right time to face up to what is behind it all. I'm sure, as I tried to free myself from depression, that I wanted to change, but I'm not sure that I understood why I should or what to change to, and I certainly didn't understand how to change, even if I had had the time to think about it, which I didn't. There were the diapers to wash (disposables in those days leaked and it got everywhere), the next feed to do, the baby clinic to go to, and so on and so on.

The Deeply Meaningful Something-or-others that I know about now were not a part of my thinking in those days. How could I face them? You cannot free yourself from something if you don't know what it is. How can any of us possibly face up to recognizing our DMSs when life is so busy, and particularly when the depression is so bad that we question our basic wish to survive? If added to that we still do not really know who we are, we are unlikely to get a grip on our DMSs and get ourselves up out of the depression.

Men fear silence as they fear solitude, because both give them a glimpse of the terror of life's nothingness.
—*André Maurois*

I only faced my DMSs with someone whom I trusted beside me, who loved me enough to listen. Someone who believed in me and also had the wisdom to help me see what was underneath it all.

Those conditions for change are not always present. Most of us concentrate only on daily survival. It's like climbing. I go up a climb as well as I can. I don't have time to worry about style or doing it by the book; I just do it. I trust the leader, and he holds the lifeline and shouts instructions. But I can't always follow as he might expect. I just *do something*.

Change is possible

Dorothy Rowe makes the point that *we are not stuck with depression forever*. We can do something about it, but we need to feel safe enough to face it all.

If we do decide we really must do something to change our situation, we also need to recognize that many of us would prefer not to. Change is almost always rather frightening.

What helps us to change?

By getting the things in our mind out where we can examine them, we can start to see what it is that makes us depressed. Tablets can never do that. However, taking some kind of medication can be a very good thing for some people.

Although I take antidepressants, I don't leave it at that. I use them as a prop to make life tolerable while I try to unravel the chaos in my mind that made me depressed in the first place. I want to know why it happened. I want to know what it is that I am really feeling. I want to stand there, poised on my toes trying to fathom out the next move. I'm less likely to fall back down the cliff if I get a firm grip and if I don't rely on being dragged up.

If I can understand what caused my depression (again), then maybe I will be less likely to become depressed again in the future, or if I do get depressed again, maybe it will not be so bad.

To find out what my DMSs are, I write in my journal. This gives me time and space to find out what is worrying me. You might prefer to paint, or play loud music, or jog around the park.

Don't be put off by the thought that finding out what is behind the depression will be a very introspective process and that this is somehow a bad thing. (See my comment in the foreword.) I'm convinced that it is better to err on the side of too much introspection in order to find out what our DMSs are. Not to understand ourselves and to remain depressed is infinitely worse than any risk of overdoing the thinking that a journal (or other creative activity) involves.

Finding time for quiet

Finding some time to ourselves in the day is a way of being quiet and listening to ourselves. We find it so hard to make the interminable racket in our minds shut down for long enough to latch on to the messages of love, peace, and beauty that can come to us from our friends, or music, or other things that we enjoy. To recover from depression we need to be quiet and to listen to ourselves, which is possible, even in this noisy world.

Much of the climb will be about discovering our inner selves, seeing our true value to our creator, and learning to love ourselves. Not a narcissistic love—"Wow, I'm the greatest"—but a true love of our selves as valuable people.

Most of my life I have needed more time to be on my own.
—P. D. James

The journey toward this understanding of our inner selves, our "heart and soul," takes many forms. I believe that relaxation and meditation can help us to get out of depression. It is not a case of meditating on "nothing"; we have to choose what to meditate on.

The collection of pictures and poems that I keep by my bed helps me. I have a beautiful modern translation of the psalms with fantastic photos that remind me of walking in the country with friends. They help me get beyond my feelings and see the beauty of the natural world. Looking at my picture of a puffin makes me think of the sea and the birds and freedom, which feels great.

My favorite picture is that of a little child protected by the hand of God. How I love that picture! I let myself feel like that little child: protected, loved, and valued.

We need this type of thing in front of us when we relax and meditate.

By choosing to be positive, we are deciding that we want to be up at the top of the cliff.

What helps?
When I look back on the things that helped me when I wrote the first edition of this book, these were:

> *my friendship with someone who accepted me unconditionally and*
> *who was prepared to sit beside me and work with me in my struggle*
> *therapy*
> *praying with someone*
> *my own determination to do things to try to get better (talking,*
> *eating well, exercising, and so on)*
> *finding time to be quiet and to be on my own*
> *deciding that I wanted to be at the top of the cliff!*

There is more about **coping strategies** in the next chapter.

Activity

- Take time to be quiet. Try the relaxation exercises in chapter 10 while listening to some beautiful music.
- If you are able to get out, go for a long walk in the country or in a park, or book an afternoon at a convent or monastery. It takes a bit of courage to make contact in the first place, but many of these places will welcome someone who just wants to sit and be quiet. You don't have to talk to anyone, and you certainly don't have to be a churchgoer.

13
Clarifying our coping strategies

If you are like me, you will read these chapters on strategies for living and say, "Yeah, yeah, yeah, I can do that." But you won't actually do anything! So when the bad times come and hit us full in the face, we aren't ready for them. Instead of handling the really bad times in a creative way, we crumple. Lethargy takes hold, and a bad day becomes an intolerable day. And those kinds of days tend to turn into intolerable weeks, maybe even months or years.

It really can help if we take time to devise our list of coping strategies, things that will help us when we think we are sitting at the foot of the cliff. And we need to put the list up where we will see it when we feel ghastly.

You are likely to know already some of the things that help you to cope:

- Phoning a friend (if you can manage to get around the fear of intruding on her time, telling yourself she doesn't really care about you and indulging in all the other negative self-talk we all use to stop ourselves from reaching out when we need to talk or have a hug).
- Finding your own personal space, going to it, and trying to relax.
- Listening to a favorite bit of music.

and so on.

Finding what works for us

My coping strategies include:

- Sitting with my teddies, watching a favorite video.
- Going to bed when I've had quite enough of a horrible day.
- Making a cup of tea.
- Eating chocolate.
- Walking where I can see flowers, birds, and butterflies. (I find this sense of connecting with nature and the universe crucial; it enables me to feel a part of something wonderful.)
- Cuddling my little dog, Alice, and playing her favorite games.
- Looking at my vegetable garden and letting myself feel the wonder of creation.
- Doing something creative, such as sewing part of a patchwork quilt for a friend.
- Writing in my journal.
- Looking at my posters and the pictures on my wall: puffins; a penguin sitting in a crevasse at the South Pole saying "If this is the first day of the rest of my life, I'm in a lot of trouble."

The problem, of course, is that when we feel we are at the foot of the cliff, we feel so overwhelmed, so desperate, so utterly worthless, that finding any motivation to do any of these things is very difficult! We are much more likely to sit and mope, crying at the hopelessness of it all, and saying "no" to all the kind suggestions from anyone trying to care for us—should we be fortunate to have someone who loves us enough to do that.

But I have found that the devastatingly bad days are fewer and farther apart as time goes on. When we recognize our lack of motivation and then challenge it by *doing one small thing*, we can transform what could have been an excruciatingly painful day into one that we survive reasonably well because we are getting better at using our coping strategies.

Devising our own list of coping strategies

In workshops over the last few years I've asked people to make lists of their coping strategies. You might want to create your own list, taking ideas from here along with others you can think of.

- Get some exercise; it makes us feel better.
- Go outside into the fresh air and sunshine (apparently in our attempts to prevent skin cancer we are not getting enough vitamin D from sunshine).
- Pay attention to nature: try tree spotting, learning about wild flowers, etc.
- Buy a light box if winter is a time when you often feel depressed.
- Make something for others.
- Watch films and read books that make you laugh.
- Set yourself simple goals and reward yourself when you achieve them.
- Make lists and check items off as you accomplish them.
- Join a self-help group (online can work just as well as face-to-face).
- Keep in touch with friends.
- If you have a good doctor, try to see him or her regularly.
- Put some structure into your life: discuss with any caregiver you might have how you can gradually take more responsibility for your life, for instance, for feeding the cat.
- Keep a list of emergency numbers by the phone and use them, so you develop your own emergency support network.
- Start a new hobby.

- If you feel isolated and lonely, decide to *do something* that will get you out of the house: volunteer at a charity thrift shop, take a class on something you have always wanted to do such as painting, singing, or auto mechanics.
- Decide to be happy.

Longer-term plans for coping

Some of the things that help us cope with really bad episodes might require a bit more time and thought to prepare.

- Make a creativity box or have things ready on a desk, for example, paints and paper, scrapbooks and photo albums, cross-stitch, woodwork, and so on. If things are more or less ready to use, you are much more likely simply to sit down and open the box and do something than you would be if you have to spend time getting things ready.
- Eat well; our bodies just cannot cope with junk food. Unless we eat properly we are just making our depression worse. If we don't have enough zinc, for example, we can be prone to mood swings. Unless we get enough vitamin C and fiber, we are likely to feel tired. So some of our depression may be due to an unhealthy diet.
- Start exercising more seriously: use the stairs instead of the escalator, walk the kids to school rather than driving, walk around the block every morning, gradually getting faster, then walk two blocks, and so on.
- Try to keep some record of how you feel on the bad days and what you did a few days before so that you can learn to spot patterns in your mood swings. I was in my midthirties before I realized that in the days immediately before my period, I became suicidal. A few years after that, my doctor suggested I try taking diuretics the week before my period. That changed my life. It appears that some of my suicide attempts were actually about my hormones. (Knowing this now for many years, I still feel weird about it. I think that is a mixture of being angry with doctors for not noticing the huge influence my periods had on me and being embarrassed by my inability to manage my life very well and my drastic behavior.)

You will see that many of my coping strategies are about opening myself up to see the beauty of the world. I find that by focusing on the glory of creation, whether it is watching an earthworm escape from a mole—which I observed to my astonishment last week—or sitting and listening to the sound of the sea, I "come out of myself" and am able to discern my place within the grand design of the universe.

Activity

Make a list of actions that you could persuade yourself to take on the very worst days. It might look something like this:

- Get up.
- Put the radio on.
- Make a hot drink.
- Eat something that is good for you, such as yogurt or fruit.
- Sit down and make a list of what you must do that day, and things that you could do. Keep all of this realistic! "Breathe in and out" is a better task for the list than "tidy the whole house!"
- Do some gentle exercise and/or stretching, or dance for twenty minutes to your favorite music.
- Plan a treat for when you have done the things on your "must-do" list.
- Make sure you give yourself some quality time to look after yourself.
- Ring one person in your self-help group.
- Prepare a survival list for the bad days. Put pictures, tapes, or whatever in a place where you can get to them easily (in a briefcase, pocket, or bag, or on the mirror in the bathroom).

This section has been about some of the things that the climb up the cliff will involve. It's not an easy journey. We are often tempted to give up. But the only way to make life any different is to decide to go for it. Ready?

Rock bottom is not a nice place to live. But we have the consolation of knowing that there is only one way to go, and that is up.
—*Ivy Rawkin Jeffers*

Part 4
First Steps

14

How can I get started?

Hope means to keep living
Amid desperation
And to keep humming
In the darkness.
—*Henri Nouwen*

In one mental hospital where I stayed for a tedious three months, there was a nurse called Frank who would often try to get us to talk about our subconscious. I used to tell him that that was impossible, because if I could talk about it, it wouldn't be subconscious, would it? In this hospital you were expected to swallow your pills and behave well at ECT times, but no "talking therapy" was used.

Frank, though, believed in the power of talking, and because of this he was frequently unpopular with staff and patients. He would often convince me that I wanted to talk to him, but as soon as I started getting rattled by something that I talked about or showed the slightest sign of crying (a rather common feature of my life), he would dose me with such a monster handful of tranquilizers that I felt ill for a week.

There was also a fascinating occupational therapist called Mary. She was as determined that I was going to join in her jolly "let's do something" sessions as I was determined that I wasn't. She thought my poetry terrible, and I thought her basket weaving and badminton outside in the wind extremely stupid. But one day she got out the paints and huge sheets of paper, and I wanted to sit and paint all afternoon. Frank wanted us to "paint depression." This was typical of him, and most of the patients became puzzled and started to wander off.

I could see, though, that the talking Frank encouraged was getting at something that the Big White Chief doctor with his electric buzz machine and his crates of tablets could never understand or get near to.

So I tried to resist the urge to retreat to my room at the thought of "painting depression," and I sat for a while, trying to work out what

Frank and Mary meant. Just three of us patients remained at the painting table nervously protesting that we didn't know what to do.

Painting depression

Gradually we mixed our colors and tried things out. We threw our first attempts away and sank into silence. I can remember the feel of that silence and being able to reach down into some part of me that I was not aware of. I remember asking myself what I *wanted* to paint. Having had a quite wonderful art teacher at school, I knew it was important to paint something that mattered to me at that moment.

Elsie was painting flowers because they made her feel happy and reminded her of life as a child. Mark was painting his house because he wanted to go home.

I couldn't settle on anything. I shut out Frank's questions and proddings and tried to think of what it was inside me that I could express in painting. It felt as if everything was shrouded in darkness, so I began to paint darkness. I realized that I just wanted to paint in black. I was embarrassed by this. Somehow I wanted to paint a black hole. I wanted to paint nothingness. I wanted to try to get this devastating isolation out onto paper.

It felt as if the end of the world had come. I remember sitting weeping helplessly on the end of the bed, feeling more ill than I had ever felt in my life, and quite unable to face the thought of anything, or to cope with my father's death and possibly another miscarriage. I just wanted to be dead myself.
—*Susan Hill*

So I covered the whole paper in black. Then I tried again and painted huge black swirls covering most of the paper except a tiny hole in the middle. Annette, my best friend on the ward, who had come back to join us by then, was sharing my pot of black and painting huge figures on her paper. Frank was trying to talk to us, but neither of us would come out of our black holes. We just painted silently.

I sat for ages trying to work out if I wanted to put anything in my tiny little hole in the middle. I liked it empty because that was how it felt, a huge black hole with just a tiny speck of light. But I felt that wasn't exactly right, so I tried some other pictures. I did a deep, dark pit with me sitting at the bottom, unable to get out (all in black), and then another that was meant to be my children but ended up as a depiction of outer space. I knew all the time that I had to go back to my tiny hole in the earlier painting.

It took a long time to work out what that hole needed. In the end I added a very simple Christian symbol, a cross. That felt right. It was a horrible dark hole, from which there seemed no way out. But I had some vague hope in a God somewhere up there. If all that stuff I learned about at school meant anything, that was God's big moment to do something. I didn't know what I expected to happen, but that painting meant so much to me.

Still some hope?

That painting showed me that at least I still had hope. It wasn't a hope in myself. It certainly wasn't a hope in the hospital or in Frank and his little chats about the subconscious. It was vague and intangible. I still felt utterly isolated, but there was the cross.

As I sat in silence beside my painting, I could see that I had made some kind of progress that afternoon. I understood myself and the depression a bit better. It was an enormous relief.

Frank then decided it was the moment to interpret our paintings. He said that my black hole showed that there were "religious overtones" in my life and that because I had left that little hole in the middle, it showed that I wasn't really all that depressed! Annette's paintings were similarly subjected to this artistic criticism.

We both started to laugh, which just made Frank more bossy and (we thought) even more "Freudian." Mary told us to clean up while Frank continued to discuss my painting with her. I didn't want them to; I had painted a bit of me onto that paper. I had tried to communicate. I now felt exposed and vulnerable.

I started to sob as I washed up the brushes. I wouldn't have painted anything if I had known it would get discussed in this way. I was embarrassed enough as it was that I had put that cross in the hole. Why did they have to talk about it that way?

Doing something is important

I learned something that day about expressing feelings during depression. Writing, or talking, or painting, or whatever it is that grabs us (even Mary's wretched basket weaving too, I suppose) is very, very important. These activities can give us ways of expressing ourselves without using words. When feelings are locked up inside us, they cramp our style for the climb. *If we can get those feelings out into the open, we have much more chance of understanding them and freeing ourselves from them.* I discovered that some of those feelings were positive. I had some kind of hope. I hadn't realized that.

> **We should not let our fear hold us back from pursuing our hopes.**
> —*John F. Kennedy*

Expressing feelings can be dangerous

I learned too that externalizing our feelings can be rather dangerous. What we feel when we are depressed is very personal. It is vital to understand what is going on inside us. However, the person or persons to whom we show our feelings must be trustworthy and able to control their own opinions so that the depressed person feels safe enough to go on exploring those feelings. I thought that I trusted Frank, but his dissection of my painting left me distinctly uneasy.

The next week when we did painting again, Annette and I fooled around, painting a huge mural of our worst nightmares and then trying to paint into the picture all the faces of the staff and patients. Word got around, and patients came to sit for a portrait.

I painted Frank with a wagonload of tranquilizers. The previous week, when he had finally finished his brushstroke by brushstroke analysis of my paintings, I tore them all up and threw them into the trash. He had retorted with such a massive dose of Valium that I can remember my room swimming around me before I had a chance to get myself into bed. But I remembered that cross I had painted. It was to be one of the turning points in my climb out of depression.

> **Hope has two lovely daughters, anger and courage.**
> —*Augustine of Hippo*

15

What preparations can I make?

**Creativity is the successful resolution of
internal conflict.**
—*A psychiatrist*

Somehow, however painful or impossible, or however much of a waste
of time it seems, I must make the decision to climb up or life will stay
this terrible. Of course terrible lethargy and hopelessness will strike!
"What's the point . . . ?"

Once you have made the decision to try to climb up out of
depression, there are a few things you can do to get ready for the
climb. Having been through many phases of depression, I have learned
that if I sit around waiting for it all to get better, I will have a very long
wait. So you need to make a start with something.

How do we start?

• with something small
• with just one thing
• with some kind of "action plan"

Although taking some action is essential for the climb out of
depression, the beginning of your action plan needs to be realistic. It's
best to sit at the foot of the cliff or on some safe ledge until you feel fit
and ready. This is important preparation time. It is a time of making
your resolve and planning your ascent.

One step at a time

Trying to do too much at the same time is no good. I find that although
it seems painfully slow to me, I must tackle one thing at a time. I never
get anywhere when I write in my journal about my need to be more
outgoing. Yuk! It's far too general, so enormous and overwhelming, and

the thought of it so terrifying, that I give up before I start. But, if I tell myself that I could manage to go out tonight or phone that one person to see how she is, I can cope, because these are small, manageable tasks.

Don't worry about the overhang ahead

In climbing, it is important to take just one small step at a time, the one that's directly in front of you at the moment. It's not that we shouldn't think about the future—clearly we must plan for some things—but if we worry about the overhang ahead, we will not be concentrating on what needs attention right now. If we don't concentrate, we will fall.

So when depression strikes, and the thought of the whole day ahead or of what must be done tomorrow or next week brings total panic, just concentrate on the next ten seconds. When you have grasped those ten seconds, you may find you can contemplate the next ten minutes. In the bad times I try never to think too much beyond the next ten minutes; doing so would send me into total panic. Then when I've finished contemplating that ten minutes, I tell myself how well I did it. Now I can think about the next ten minutes. Eventually I conclude that maybe life is not that bad . . . today. Maybe I can manage it. So maybe I can think of going to the shop to get some milk.

Doing a little bit every day

Climbing out of depression is like keeping the kitchen tidy or keeping the house from looking like the storeroom of the local thrift shop. Doing a little bit every day is the key.

When I am teaching, I promise myself to tidy my desk every day before I go home. However bad life gets at work (and it can be devastatingly awful for teachers), those few minutes pay off. If I let myself look around the classroom and think of all there is to do, I might be so overcome by it all that I do nothing!

Depression is just like life itself in that way: It is so big, so overwhelming, so mysterious, and so irritatingly difficult to get a grip on, that I can easily give up in the attempt. The only way to proceed is to face a little bit of it at a time. When we deal with it in little chunks, we can achieve some success. *Succeeding at anything is a terrific antidote to depression!*

It looks worse from down here than it really is

Standing at the foot of the cliff, looking up, gives us a very distorted view of what it is actually like. Every lump looks like a gigantic overhang. The tiny crevices seem far too small to offer a foot- or handhold. The more we look, think, and worry the more impossible it seems. Before we get into a total panic, we need to get the lifeline on, check to make sure our helmet is fastened, and make a start.

Exercise, creativity, and diet

There is a close relationship between the state of the physical body and the state of the mind. We will recover from depression much more quickly if we also take care of our bodies. People who sit indoors all day, doing very little and eating all sorts of things that are "bad" for them, are likely to feel depressed.

When I notice the telltale signs of early depression, I have learned to put myself on a rigid diet and set out on a gentle but increasingly vigorous exercise program. I really do feel better on days when I eat fresh fruit and vegetables and go out for a walk than on days when I sit at home and eat chocolate and go to bed for the afternoon.

However, as I came to write the second edition of this book, I read an article about a "rigid diet," and I realized that although I might have once been able to do that, I don't think I did it very well. My eating has been chaotic since childhood. Sometimes I starve myself, once becoming dangerously underweight. Sometimes I binge (like yesterday), feeling so ill I vow I will never do it again. I used to make myself sick, but I've promised myself I will never do that again. (*Hmm!*)

I am what the world calls a "yo-yo dieter." After every really good phase of getting my body mass index to a healthy level (ask your doctor or the gym about this), I then gradually put all the weight back on and usually a bit more! So over the last thirty years, my weight has crept up and up.

I *know* I need to replace dieting with "healthy eating," but I don't actually behave as if I believe that. So one of the things that I'm working at on my "word wall" is keeping my body healthy so I can see my children and grandchildren grow up and enjoy an active life with my husband, David.

Caring for our body

On some days we are likely to find that retreating to bed is all that we can do. On some days, some of us would argue, we *need* to eat chocolate! (Hell has no chocolate.) But I am saying that a part of our recovery is getting our bodies gradually fitter. This makes us feel better about ourselves. We need to take care of our bodies; they are the only ones we have, and getting spares is very complicated.

Physical exercise

When we do something that requires physical exertion, we awaken a part of ourselves that otherwise lies dormant. This can develop a feeling of well-being.

Apparently, exercise triggers the release in the brain of substances called "endorphins," which create a sense of well-being. I can certainly vouch for the fact that when I do something physical, I feel better. It improves my mood and reduces my anxiety.

It doesn't have to be something extremely energetic like swimming or jogging. Just a few stretching exercises in the bedroom, cleaning part of the house, or five minutes dancing to music (with the blinds pulled down to stop the neighbors from thinking we've finally flipped!) can be enough to lift our spirits. A walk to the local market for some bread can be the thing that will get us out of the "slough of despond" some days. The important thing is to find out what works for us and when.

The trouble is that terrible lethargy strikes. We look at the dust. We think of all the jobs that need doing. We don't know where to start. So we have another cup of tea and decide that we will leave cleaning the windows until we "feel like it."

That's just how depression is. It doesn't seem worth cleaning the house; it will just get dirty again. We seem to drift through the day getting little done. We look at the dust again. Maybe tomorrow. But tomorrow will be the same unless we make a start.

Making a start with some exercise

If you are not used to exercise or if you are over thirty-five, check with your doctor first.

- Don't start with anything extreme. Start gently and work your way up very slowly. If you overdo it, you will ache all over, perhaps injure yourself, and give up.
- Do gentle warm-up exercises to start with, then remember to do cool-down stretches at the end. This stops your muscles from complaining too much.
- Choose something that suits your lifestyle and that you could come to enjoy doing. Dancing, brisk walking, swimming, and jogging are all activities we can do on our own. Some people get more out of exercise if they join a local gym or a tennis club, or do something with a friend.
- You need to work up to about twenty minutes of exercise at a time. This may take several weeks. Twenty minutes seems to be enough to get those messages of well-being to our brain and to get our hearts doing the things that doctors tell us they should be doing. But if you get breathless or feel some pain, stop. I've built up from twenty minutes to an hour and a quarter in the gym about twice a week. On days in between, I do shorter sessions at home. (At least this is what I tell myself I do!)
- Keep some sort of note of what you do. It really helps your sense of progress. I write down briefly what I have done on a spare calendar, so yesterday's entry read: "Swam 20 mins." If I do this I can see that I am building up strength and stamina, and that I am doing something about three or four times a week.
- Don't exercise if you feel ill, or on days when you suspect you may be coming down with something; it will only make you take three steps backward.

Doing something creative

Something creative, such as writing, sewing, painting, or singing, makes us feel better. All the depressed people I know agree on that.

Here is a quick list of creative things to do—and there are other suggestions throughout the book.

- Make a happy book (you can write only happy thoughts in it).
- Make a special box to keep cards and important mementos.
- Write poetry.
- Take up photography.
- Learn to fold paper into shapes (origami).

- Go sit in a children's library and find books you used to read.
- Start a neighborhood newspaper or book group.
- Write a letter or an article for *A Single Step*, the magazine published by Depression Alliance, or for websites about depression (see the resource list for useful addresses). Sharing your perceptions could give someone the strength to keep going that day. Maybe it will spread hope, which is something we desperately need when we are at the foot of the cliff.

Doing something—it doesn't matter too much what—will reinforce your decision to take the first step into reality. When the physical and the creative come together we can get great benefit from the combination. Maybe that is why gardening is such a popular hobby. People may not need to grow cabbages or peas to survive; they grow them because they enjoy growing them. It's great fun to buy a packet of seed in the spring, hack away at barren earth, and then experience the joy of seeing the green shoots appear. Gardening makes me feel that God and I are working together on something, and that makes me feel good. I do get horribly murderous thoughts about rabbits, pigeons, and slugs, though. Why do they always eat my baby plants and seem not to touch Ted's next door? It could be that I'm just being paranoid, but it's true: The world, and especially the rabbits, are against me!

> **Those who sow in tears**
> **will reap with songs of joy.**
> —*The Psalmist*

Psychologists and psychiatrists argue about how much body chemistry influences depression. I'm not qualified to comment because I don't understand it. What I do know is that there are some things (medication, diet, exercise, and so on) that can influence the way we think.

Herbal teas help me to sleep. Avoiding coffee helps me not to tremble. Chewing sugar-free gum helps me cope with nausea. Exercise makes me feel good. State of mind and state of body are very closely linked.

There are some things about depression that, for some, will need more than the home remedies I describe in this book. Going into the hospital or being a day patient can seem very drastic, but the routine of the day and having no responsibilities (which helps you to concentrate on what it is that is bugging you) can be very calming and reassuring.

Some people recover from depression after being hospitalized for occupational therapy treatment and doing craft work. For other people, being forced to sit there every Tuesday and Thursday morning is practice for hell.

It's a case of finding out what works for you. Write down in your journal what it was about a day that made it almost tolerable. That way you will find out what things help you to feel better.

Having a good diet

The decision to start the climb must be based on fitness. Last summer I didn't go out with my friends on one climb because I felt ill. It would have made it tough going and spoiled the rest of the holiday. It's like that for us on the climb up from depression. If we are unfit, we will climb badly. We'll be more likely to fall and as a result lose our confidence.

Those who have gotten better from depression recognize the importance of having a good diet. And "real" food is better than processed or convenience food.

Many experts agree that a good diet is one that is:

- low in fat—preferably polyunsaturated (such as olive oil or sunflower margarine) rather than animal fats
- high in fiber—lots of vegetables, whole grains, and cereals, such as wheat, oats, and rice
- as varied as possible, so it includes a full range of vitamins and minerals—foods such as muesli and mixed salads are ideal
- low in sugar and salt

Watch out for those misleading labels such as "lower fat," "low-cal," or "only natural colorings." This last label in particular might make you think that such products, often sweets or so-called fruit drinks, might be all right for your children, but they will still be so packed full of sugar that they are far from healthy.

The level of obesity is rising in line with products that tempt us to believe we can eat them freely! Read the labels on things that tell us they are "healthy options" to be sure that they really are.

The "good enough" diet

For most of us, getting a good diet has to be some form of compromise.

- Convenience foods give us the extra time that we need to survive depression, motherhood, the rigors of working, or the fact that preparing a meal drives us crazy. (But beware of processed foods; these tend to have additives and preservatives that can make us feel unwell.)
- Treats (such as chocolate or a take-out meal) make us feel happy and relaxed.
- Some "good" food (such as quality whole-wheat bread) is much more expensive than mass-produced equivalents, so sometimes we need to buy just what we can afford.

Our diet just needs to be "good enough."

Activity

- Make an "action plan." Keep it realistic!
- Keep a diary of exercise and what you eat.
- The diary can focus you on the times when you are likely to eat "bad" things.
- A diary provides an overall sense of progress.

One who recovers from sickness forgets about God.
—*Ethiopian proverb*

16

Things we need to take

He is a man who is impossible to please because he is never pleased with himself.
—*Goethe*

One of the obvious things about climbing is that you need to be dressed for the job. You would hardly set off wearing a bikini and plastic beach sandals and carrying a suitcase stuffed with your items for the week. But some people attempt to get through life ill equipped and carrying all sorts of unnecessary and unhelpful "luggage" with them. We will look at some of the things we need to leave behind (chapter 18), but in this chapter we will look at some of the things we need to take with us: the gear.

Putting on the right gear

Climbing gear is always minimal but essential. As with our "gear" for life, it isn't the quantity that is important; it's the way we use what we have.

Preparation for climbing is thorough, and it is only when essential items such as belts, harnesses, and helmets have been checked and the lifeline ropes have been carefully anchored, that the leader will go ahead. As a member of the team I have no choice in this. I obey the rules, or I don't climb.

What do we need for the climb? Our "essential gear" might be:

a willingness to work at change

a refusal to accept society's stigma of "mental illness"

a good friend, therapist, doctor, minister, or some other caregiver
  who will listen to us

some medication, if that's what the doctor recommends

an action plan for working on understanding ourselves
    (for example, working through the activities in this book)

a personal journal

Keeping a journal

Even if we hate writing, most of us are self-centered enough to get something out of writing about ourselves. It can be a most effective way to set about understanding the climb ahead. If we keep even the briefest of jottings in our journal, over the months we may see that there are similarities in our experiences.

Here are some examples:

Every time you go to your in-laws you get a headache.

Driving on the highway makes you feel tense.

Eating out late makes you unable to sleep.

Drinking red wine makes you feel ill.

You feel more depressed in the winter than in the spring and summer.

On the anniversary of a death you suffer panic attacks.

Gardening makes you feel better.

Just before your monthly period you are tense and totally unreasonable.

The day after exercise is usually a good one.

We need to learn how we tick. Some things are quite easy to work out; others are more complex.

Why does that irritating habit she has drive me up the wall?

What is it about that person's death that leaves me so devastated?

What is it about society's attitude toward women that makes me so angry?

What is it about food that makes me pig out so much?

In our journals we can try to look for common themes, the things that crop up time after time and are obviously going to be important in our climb out of depression.

Working with a friend

When you find a pattern, try to determine its origin. It's not easy, and it may take many weeks to figure it out. It is helpful to find someone with whom we can share some of our insights.

Work toward talking with someone. Maybe join a self-help group.

74

Various organizations run self-help groups or drop-in centers where people can go and just "be." Some groups are specific, such as those for parents at home with babies. Many are run by people who are, or who have been, depressed themselves. (See the resources list at the back for useful addresses.)

Maybe you would get a great deal from doing the activities in this book with someone else who is depressed.

Life is a story

Writing in a journal or talking with others is partly about telling ourselves our own story. This is one way to come to terms with our life and free ourselves from the trap of despair. We begin to open up possibilities of seeing beyond our tight little lives into what could be and what might be. It's something of an adventure to start taking those first steps out of depression. All adventures are a bit scary.

Adventure is the meeting of dreams and realities.

Activity: the journal

- Writing "Top Secret—Do Not Read" on the cover is asking for trouble!
- Dates are important for looking back. There may be some regular pattern in our depressed feelings.
- How often you write will be a reflection of your feelings. Sometimes I write in my journal several times a day. Sometimes I add nothing to it for weeks on end.
- Sketches, pictures stuck in, newspaper clippings, family photos, and so on all help to capture your thoughts and feelings. (I keep a picture of a puffin in mine, because it reminds me of the beauty of God's creation, the freedom of the sea, and how utterly fantastic puffins are. There was a time when I was so depressed that I thought I would die, but when I saw a puffin, I felt, quite suddenly and unexpectedly, that everything would be okay.)
- The main purpose of a journal is to help us to understand ourselves better, to take a firmer grip on the rock face, and therefore to make the rest of the climb much more straightforward and less painful. (Eventually!)

I've got the gear on, now what?

So you have struggled into the various bits of gear ready for a climb, and you're standing at the foot of the cliff feeling like a trussed turkey and wishing you had gone to the bathroom before you put it all on. This is when it all really begins. Climbing isn't just about the gear—helmets and ropes and harnesses—there are three other vital ingredients:

- your own grit and determination
- the rest of the team
- a trustworthy leader

> **Surprise yourself every day with your own courage.**
> —*Denholm Elliott*

17
Life is difficult

**Seek not abroad, turn back into thyself,
for in the inner man dwells the truth.**
—*Augustine of Hippo*

Your own grit and determination will, in the end, be one of the main ingredients in the success of the climb. Anyone who has suffered from depression and has survived the experience long enough to try to do something about it—such as reading a book about it, as you are now—has the makings of a successful climber.

Those who tell us how good they are at things, or those who get easily to the top, or those who seem to sail through life as if it were one long party, do not necessarily have true grit and courage.

When I watch children at school on the jungle gym, it's not the child who goes straight to the top and stands there looking confident who is the one with courage. It's the little child who has just come to school and who climbs up slowly and cautiously, sometimes losing her footing. This child may not even get to the top. Perhaps she goes halfway and then turns around and gives the teacher a timorous smile. I see myself in that kind of child. She will get there one day, and it will be all the more important because it took time, a few bruises, and a great deal of guts.

Climbing is difficult

At the beginning of his book *The Road Less Traveled,* M. Scott Peck makes the observation that "life is difficult." That seems to me to be a realistic starting point from which to view our climb. If we develop a view that somehow life should be calm, easy, delightful, and trouble-free at all stages, we are in for a shock!

The climb ahead of everyone is difficult. Even when we are fit, healthy, well off, at peace with ourselves, and terribly happy, there are difficulties to face.

There are stages in our lives when we cannot get through the day without being scratched, battered, and bruised. It's like those stretches of a rock climb where there is nothing to hold on to, no other way up other than putting your hand right into a crevice and making a fist that jams tight, giving you enough of a hold to pull yourself up. You leave rather a lot of yourself behind on the rock face, and it is terribly painful. You just have to not think about it. If you want to get up, it will be worth it in the end.

A lot of life seems to be about blood, sweat, and tears. The moments in history that stick in our minds are moments of great triumph that often were accomplished only by the shedding of blood, the loss of life, or by someone giving all to achieve something. Michelangelo didn't get that ceiling in the Sistine Chapel done overnight. Human rights for minorities have cost a lot of lives and no doubt will cost more. It seems impossible therefore, even in our very ordinary lives, to doubt that one of the crucial parts of our survival strategy for our climb should be preparing ourselves for getting hurt or rejected.

Life is difficult. At times very, very difficult. It takes a lot of courage to face it.

It's okay to go backward

Many times when I am climbing across a rock face, my moves to find a better hold involve going back or sideways. This sideways movement is called "traversing" by the leader. He isn't just being polite. It really is okay when climbing to come back down a bit, then go sideways. In fact, sometimes that is the best way to climb. But that's not how society usually sees it.

The values of our society

The values of the society in which I live seem to have become very competitive. I haven't studied enough history to know how that came about. Some people have told me that competitiveness is "basic to human nature." Is it? When I climb I experience something like "success" and "getting to the top," but it isn't from competition. It's a team effort as well as an individual's achievement for its own sake that is not measured against anyone else's efforts.

So much of society seems to value success in a different way:

- The only thing that matters in life is to Get On.
- Your personal value is measured by your degree of success, which in turn is measured by how far up the ladder you have climbed (and sometimes by how many people you managed to knock off on the way).
- You are measured by the amount of money you earn.

The education system sometimes gives out the message that the only thing that matters is to pass exams and get into college. Those children who do not manage to do so often assume they are no good and useless. They do not see their value as human beings. Those who do, often feel the need to go on succeeding in everything all through life.

> **If a child lives with approval, he learns to live with himself.**
> —*Dorothy Law Nolte*

When I was just a mother at home (note how that word "just" creeps in), I almost felt I had to justify my existence to some people. For some reason I found this worst at dinner parties. People would peer at me and say, "And what do you do?" "I'm a mother," I would say, and a great silence would follow. I let this develop over the years into "I'm doing the most important job in the world: raising children." Not all were convinced.

To be anyone worthwhile I had to be "someone": a secretary or a nurse, anything. It is exactly that attitude that works against our building up our self-esteem. Life isn't measured by what we do but by who we are. That terrible cliché contains another one of those Great Truths. I don't think God gives out points for what jobs we do: five thousand for a brain surgeon and three if you screw the tops on tubes of toothpaste. But that's often how society makes us feel. (You get only one point if you work at home doing the cleaning and the wiping of snotty noses.)

And it is exactly this attitude that we pick up that contributes to our depression.

Getting a realistic view of what our problem really is

In addition to the negative attitudes of others, those who are depressed often do not value themselves very much. Having a low self-image is very, very common indeed among depressed people. It shows itself in the things that we say: "I'm useless," "I'm ugly," "Everything I do fails," "I can't do anything about it."

This affects the way we look after ourselves and the way we dress. What's the point in brushing my hair? Why wear nice clothes? None of that will do any good.

This lack of care for ourselves can mean that we do not eat well, or exercise, and perhaps abuse our bodies with too much medication, alcohol, smoking, or other drugs. When all this is linked with the sleep problems of being depressed it is little wonder that we feel so ill!

Man is what he believes.
—*Anton Chekhov*

It's best to climb with others

One of the very best things about rock climbing is the companionship of others who want to do the same. We all encourage and help one another. No one thinks any less of me when I can't get up a climb. We're all in it together, and shared successes (and failures) are what holds us together as a group and the stuff of hugs and tears.

Not only is it more fun in a group, but it is also very much safer. It's just plain stupid to set out on our own. The trouble is that we can feel so alone during depression that we cannot sense the companionship that may be there. Loneliness is one of the hardest things to deal with in life.

Sometimes, when things get very bad, we feel we need someone to help us urgently and desperately (and it gets very desperate at times), but we feel unfit to face anyone. ("They won't want to bother with me.") That's low self-esteem. If you knew someone was desperate for help, you wouldn't want them not to ask, would you? Our caregivers can sometimes be upset by our inability to accept their concern.

It's hard to ask though, and the best way to resolve this type of problem may be to join a self-help group. There is a list of organizations you can contact at the end of the book.

Helpers get it wrong
Many of the people who set out to help us inevitably get it all wrong.

- They ask us questions ("Are you okay?" "Do you want a cup of tea?"), and we hate that because we cannot make decisions.
- They cook our favorite meal, but if we are off food at that moment we burst into tears.
- They tidy the kitchen, and we feel threatened because it may be a subtle way of telling us that they wish we would keep the place neater.
- They put fresh flowers in the hall, and we cry because they will die there.
- They suggest (in great kindness) that we get a new coat, and we think it means we should do something about our disheveled appearance.

Of course they will get it wrong. Depression is so incomprehensible, individual, and isolating that they can hardly do otherwise.

Working with our caregivers
One of the most noticeable features of doing workshops on depression with counselors is their nervousness about what to say to depressed people. This is completely understandable! I know I can be very edgy when I am depressed and poor David, my husband, tries so hard to be kind and reasonable.

If we are to make the most of any care that comes our way, we do need to try to think about what our caregivers are trying to do and why it is so hard for them.

- It is scary to see someone you love in so much pain.
- There can be the worry about suicide.
- If they have never encountered depression before, they may think we can just pull ourselves together, or they might lose patience with us (quite a reasonable thing to happen) and then feel guilty that they haven't really found a way to help us.

There are probably many other things that caregivers find frustrating and inexplicable.

We need to be kind to them!

We need to talk through what we are both feeling with them.

Moving on

When I have tried to care for people who are feeling really low, I find it extraordinarily difficult. Years ago I would have thought that I might be quite good at it, but I'm not. I sometimes get far too involved with people. I begin to feel panicky myself. I dread the next phone call or email. But I'm getting much better at it. And I'm quite sure it is true that once we have recovered a little from our depression, we can be a crucial part of the recovery of other depressed people.

- We know what they are going through.
- We can turn our pain into "being there" for someone still at the foot of the cliff.

Think:

- How can I help someone who is depressed?
- How can I be kind to my caregiver?

Is the leader reliable enough?

The leader is crucial to the success of any rock climb. It matters whom you listen to and whom you model your life on. The leader teaches you the rules of climbing—and there are lots of them—which make life easier, such as keeping your body away from the rock so that you can see what you're doing and gain better balance. Above all, when you learn to climb, you learn to listen to the leader.

Our leader

The people whom we counted as our leaders when we were children (parents, teachers, aunts, grandparents, and so on) sometimes expected us to make the climb quite ill equipped. Indeed, for many of us it felt as if some people were concentrating hard on stamping on our fingers just as we thought we had found a handhold. They seemed not to care about holding the lifeline when we thought they were. They wandered off, just when we needed them, leaving us exposed and in danger.

Some of these people were not good leaders, and, when we followed their example, we scrabbled up the cliff using any technique we could think of. We got horribly injured as we did so and increasingly frantic as we felt ourselves slipping. If all we have known is this ill-equipped scrabbling at life, our choices are too restricted for us to be able to make rational and sensible life-saving ones.

There isn't actually anything "good" about being at the foot of the cliff, but when we are on the flat stretches it is a little easier to rest and consider the options. One of these options is to think about some better equipment, to consider who might be a better leader than those we have had so far, and to make some more informed choices, painful and embarrassing though they may be.

> **And now unto Him who is able to keep us from falling and lift us from the dark valley of despair to the bright mountain of hope, from the midnight of desperation to the daybreak of joy; to Him be power and authority, for ever and ever.**
> —*Martin Luther King, Jr.*

Whom shall I choose as a leader?

Our choices of leaders profoundly influence how we climb through life. If we choose to follow and support those who live by putting others down or by violence, or those who put themselves first, it will be reflected in the way we climb.

If, on the other hand, we choose to be like those who live for others or those who work for peace and justice in this crazy world, these attitudes will become ours and influence the way we climb.

It matters whom we follow and whom we trust.

Think

- What sort of "worth" do I think people give to me and to what I do? Do I feel that people put me down or undervalue me?
- What sort of "worth" do I give myself? Do I undervalue myself?
- Who are the people whom I respect or would like to be like? List them.
- Whom do I trust to be my "leader"?

My sheep hear my voice and I know them and they follow me.
—*Jesus, in the Gospel of John*

More about **low self-esteem** in chapters 25 and 26.

18

Things to leave behind

Climbing has every kind of emotion in it.
—*Chris Bonnington, climber*

There is something wonderfully carefree about my teenagers and their friends. Despite having had me tell them for years to wrap up warm, I notice now that they go out for whole days just in the clothes that they stand up in. No jacket. Nothing for "just in case."

Although I'm not the type of person who turns up for a four-hour ramble across the local hills with enough to keep a family of five alive for a week, I was trained in the Girl Scouts to "be prepared." As a mother I learned to take Band-Aids, tissues, and so on, just for a trip to the local park. As an attitude toward life, though, I'm not sure that mine is a healthy one.

Of course, it is sensible to be prepared. But what about the things that we don't need? We don't need to go on our climb with a backpack stuffed full of things we could survive without. We get bogged down and worn out with our burden, and we would be much better without it.

That's where I think my teenagers have got it right with life. They just take themselves, a few friends, and they are off.

If I had my life to live over, I'd dare to make more mistakes next time. I'd relax. I would limber up. I would be sillier than I have been this trip. I would take fewer things seriously. I would take more chances. I would take more trips. I would climb more mountains and swim more rivers. I would eat more ice cream and fewer beans. I would perhaps have more actual troubles, but I'd have fewer imaginary ones.

You see, I'm one of those people who live sensibly and sanely hour after hour, day after day. Oh, I've had my moments, and if I had it to do over again, I'd have more of them. In fact, I'd try to have nothing else. Just moments. One after the other, instead of living so many years ahead of each day.

I've been one of those people who never goes anywhere without a thermometer, a hot-water bottle, a raincoat and a parachute. If I had to do it again, I would travel lighter.

If I had my life to live over, I would start barefoot earlier in the spring and stay that way later in the fall. I would go to more dances. I would ride more merry-go-rounds. I would pick more daisies.
—Nadine Stair, aged eighty-five

Getting rid of the backpack

In *Pilgrim's Progress,* which John Bunyan wrote in prison, Christian sets out on a journey seeking the narrow path to heaven with an enormous and heavy pack on his back. On the way, he meets various helpers who tell him about a place where he will be able to put his burdens down.

Christian searches for this place, faces many hardships, and learns many lessons along the way. One day, to his delight, he feels sure that he is close to the place he is seeking. The path becomes steep and rough and a great struggle to climb, but he is so keen to get rid of his burden that he rushes up it.

At the top of the slope he finds a simple wooden cross. He kneels at the foot of the cross, and his burden immediately falls off his back and rolls down the slope, disappearing into an open grave. Christian stands up and feels the freedom of being able to stretch and walk free of the huge load. He stands quietly for a moment, thinking of the person who died on that cross so that he can walk free: "He hath given me rest by His sorrow, and life by His death." He is so grateful that tears of joy roll down his cheeks as he thinks of that death and his own freedom. He is so thrilled that he jumps for joy and sings at the top of his voice.

This lovely image of a Christian coming to the foot of the cross and laying down his burden is a good one to meditate on. Most of us do try to lighten our load and lay our burdens down. We are good at saying "Oh God, please help me." The trouble is that we tend to kneel for a while, then at the end of our thoughts we stand up and, instead of leaving our burdens behind, we pick them up again and trudge off!

Life on the cliff face with a weighty pack on our backs is tough. It is hard to hold the rock face when all the time we are fearing that we will overbalance and topple off.

How do we learn to put down our burdens?

Work out what your burdens are. It can take some time. These "burdens" can be many different things:

Negative self-talk, e.g., "I'm no good" (see chapter 19).

A lack of understanding of ourselves.

A lack of understanding of what depression is.
An unrealistic view of what life is actually about.
Unresolved conflict in the family or at work.
Feeling so much guilt that we cannot function as free individuals.
Holding on to bitterness, or allowing jealousy to influence our
  behavior, or harboring angry thoughts about some old enemy.

Getting rid of jealousy and bitterness might just improve the quality of our lives.

Work on growing away from them

This isn't an instant thing. Some days we find that we are carrying all our burdens around. Other days we seem to be free of them for a while. It is important to be aware of those moments of respite and to be happy in them. They are previews of what life can be like at the top of the climb.

The climb out of depression is helped by cashing in on those moments when we realize we are free of our burdens for a while. This morning the dread seemed a little less. The thought of getting up was not one of total terror. Maybe today the sun will shine, and I will see the first shoots of spring.

Decide which particular bit of baggage you could unload first

No one ever got rid of depression by tackling the whole lot in one go. If you cannot face the big things yet (such as forgiving someone for some great wrong they did you) maybe you can try the easier ones, such as looking at your stress level or at how you do some things to see if you make them unnecessarily complex and difficult. For example, if making up lunch boxes for the children to take to school drives you crazy, consider doing them the night before, or (my own method) get the children to do their own.

Maybe it is the tendency toward feeling guilty that makes depressed people great worriers and sometimes compulsive workers.

When I look back on all these worries, I remember the story of the old man who said on his deathbed that he

had had a lot of trouble in his life, most of which never happened.
—*Winston Churchill*

The success of the climb depends on putting down the burdens. The activities in this book are designed to clarify what the burdens are. When we know what it is that is weighing us down, it is easier to get rid of it.

- The bitter old lady who will not let bygones be bygones develops a pointing finger. She is so determined to keep accusing that she loses her ability to get a grip on the cliff face.
- The jealous man is so preoccupied with what he hasn't got that he fails to appreciate what it is he has got. He loses the ability to feel glad because the sun is shining. He doesn't see the wonder and newness of the beginning of spring.
- The angry young woman is so busy shouting her protest that she cannot hear the words of peace she is offered.
- The man burdened by guilt fails to recognize the things about life that are meant to be fun and enjoyable. He is so busy worrying about all the guilt that he doesn't appreciate his uniqueness and value.

The silence of God has at all times been a great trial to mankind.
—*W. R. Inge, Dean of St. Paul's Cathedral, London*

Remember

- The activities in this book are not the answer to everything; they do not promise that eternal bliss is just around the corner. They are simply to help you to decide what are the right questions for you to ask about your depression.
- If something doesn't prove helpful, abandon it and try something else. If we are also able to ask ourselves why something is unhelpful, we will be a bit wiser and closer to the top of the climb.

If all else fails today, go out and pick daisies, or dance barefoot on the grass, or . . .

Activity

- Review your action plan for climbing out of depression (this is developed throughout part 4).
- Make a list of what might be the burdens that you are carrying up the climb.

I feel the capacity to care is the thing which gives life its greatest significance.
—*Pablo Casals*

19

Negative thinking

A man cannot possibly be at peace with others until he has learned to be at peace with himself.
—*Bertrand Russell*

What is low self-esteem?
Low self-esteem has many features. It is something that is often difficult for others to see in people who project a cheerful and coping self to the world. We come to recognize that inside the apparently calm, confident, or exuberant individual that we let the world see, there may be a terrified person whom we think we need to conceal.

If you believe that you are bad and unacceptable you are unable to look back at your past with pleasure and toward your future with hope. Only bad things happened to you in the past and only bad things will happen to you in the future.
—*Dorothy Rowe*

Here are some of the ways we can recognize low self-esteem:

- A lack of confidence: "I can't do that." "Everything I do goes wrong." "I failed again. I always fail. I'm no good."
- A feeling of guilt that won't go away: "It's all my fault."
- Feelings of self-hatred: "I hate myself. I'm useless."
- A poor body image: "I'm ugly." "I'm too fat/thin/tall/short." "I don't like the shape of my nose/face/hips." "The only hope for me is plastic surgery."
- "I am a hopeless and useless person."

At its very worst, people with low self-esteem believe that the world would be a better place if they were dead.

We may eventually come to recognize that it is our low self-esteem that underlies our problem of depression.

Where does low self-esteem come from?

Once the idea of perceiving ourselves as worthless failures takes hold of us, it is a struggle, sometimes a deadly one, to get rid of these thoughts. Understanding how we came to think that way can be a great help. Almost certainly we didn't come out of the womb believing that we were useless!

Criticism during childhood

In his book about depression, *Roots of Sorrow*, Dr. Richard Winter identifies one major cause of low self-esteem as heavy criticism in childhood. He says that those ". . . who think they are useless and a waste of everyone's time, have often been heavily criticised in childhood and told they are hopeless failures. Even if the displeasure is never voiced, they may be nurtured in an atmosphere of 'you are not intelligent or beautiful enough for me to be proud of you and accept you.' Without the basic need for significance being met, they grow up with an aching void within and a deep longing for approval, acceptance and love."

The inability to trust

If, during our early years, we learn that it is unwise to trust people, we learn also not to trust ourselves.

In his book *God of Surprises,* Gerard Hughes expresses this beautifully:

The greatest emotional needs in childhood are for protection and affection, for without these the child cannot learn to trust himself or anyone else. The ability to grow humanly is proportionate to our ability to trust.

Without that basic trust in ourselves, it seems that all sorts of irrational beliefs come to rest in our minds as we are cut loose in childhood and forced to find our own way up the climb. These beliefs sit in our minds and result in irrational behavior and thinking.

The tiny child who is unable to trust those around her because they do not give her unconditional love, learns to trust no one, not even herself. Here are the beginnings of depression.

Misplaced guilt

The irrational beliefs that somehow things are as bad as they are because of something that is our "fault" can grow from childhood. It is alarmingly easy for children to find themselves in a situation they cannot cope with or comprehend and to come out of it with the firm belief that they caused the problem.

- When parents argue, or if they split up, the child assumes that it is because she was naughty or that she is unloved.
- The death of someone a child knows may be perceived as having been the child's fault.

We become "blamers." It takes a while to learn that blaming, especially of the reciprocal kind—"It's your fault." "No, it's your fault."—is counterproductive. Growth comes through accepting responsibility and trying to get beyond "blame."

It is a problem that is getting worse as our culture focuses more and more on finding someone to blame for everything that goes wrong.

- We drop a can of baked beans on our foot in the supermarket. Blame someone!
- Our child falls over on a school trip to an activity center. Take the teacher to court! She should lose her job!

No one could blame a teacher or youth leader for refusing to risk taking children climbing, for example. But we do need to watch that children are given opportunities for life-enhancing experiences, risks and all. I've seen children transformed during adventure trips. They gain self-esteem, and, who knows, the experience may prevent depression and teach life skills, such as risk taking.

The growth of fear

Things that children cannot understand become the stuff of nightmares and the root of negative thinking. Children may perceive the death of a grandparent or parent not only as something that they somehow caused but also as an abandonment that they actually deserved. The idea "I must be such a bad person" begins to grow in their mind and by the time they are adolescents this has been translated into "I am such a bad person that no one will ever love me."

There may be a fear of being abandoned that permeates every aspect of life. It may show itself in perfectionism: "If I do it perfectly then they will love me." It may show itself in exhibitionism: "No one loves me, so I must draw attention to myself whenever I can."

Fear that we will be left alone, unloved, and uncared for, is a fear that can escalate out of control during depression. It is made worse because we often sleep badly and have nightmares, and because any depression tends to bring with it a sense of total alienation from everyone and everything.

If one of my greatest fears is of not being loved, whenever I'm depressed I will come to believe that that is actually the case. That is certainly what it feels like. However much those around us may believe that they are helping and caring, we cannot appreciate it because we perceive ourselves as being isolated. In the pit, cut off from all human contact. This makes the fear worse. Death seems like a good idea.

Activity

- Write your own obituary.
- Write what people might say about you at your funeral service or in a short piece in the local paper. Resist the temptation to write about how hopeless

you are! Think about the good points someone would focus on in a tribute
to you.

(This activity is from *God of Surprises* by Gerard Hughes.)

I can pardon everyone's mistakes but my own.
—Marcus Porcius Cato (234–149 B.C.)

Negative thinking

One of the things that is common among depressed people is that
when something happens we say to ourselves, "It was all my fault," "If
only she hadn't died . . ." "I should have done that differently," "What
if it all goes wrong?" "She really hates me."

This is negative thinking and the what-ifs and if-onlys can rule our
lives and ruin any effective plans for recovering from depression.

One way to spot this type of thinking (and most people do it from
time to time) is to write down what we are thinking when something
goes wrong or upsets us. It may be that our depression has made this
type of negative thinking such a habit and so powerful that it is the
very thing keeping us depressed.

Sometimes it is hard to identify negative thinking. We have had a
lifetime to get it down to a fine art. We need to practice both
identifying and changing it. I carried various charts in my pocket and
used them to work on my thinking for a few weeks. I was astonished at
how much I thought in this negative way, and I was equally surprised
to find that I could change it.

I really did! I changed the way that I was thinking!

Activity

This activity helps us to learn one very significant thing about depression:
Things are not usually as bad as we think they are. What a crucial lesson
that is!

The activity uses the threefold structure explained in the foreword:

• Monitoring what we are thinking and doing.
• Analyzing the information to see if we can spot patterns.
• Acting on what we find out and making appropriate changes.

This activity is very like the process of action research as well as the professional development that I work on with teachers. I found it exciting to see where my professional life met my climb out of depression.

As with any kind of change, you need to *do* the activity, not just read it through! You might think it is utterly stupid, but all with whom I've used it, even the deeply skeptical, in the end admitted that it changed their life—okay, sometimes it was just a tiny change—but that's where we all start.

1. Read all the way through this activity.
2. Make blank copies of the chart with just the headings, leaving out the example fill-ins.
3. Put one or more charts in your bag or pocket with a pencil, and when the dreaded negative thinking hits, try to find a moment to use it.
4. You are likely to need to do a few charts to begin to see patterns that you can analyze. It is that analysis that will help us to see what is trapping you in the negative thinking that is fueling your depression. You will be able to see how you can behave, think, and feel differently if you act on what you learn. You will be able to change, and that is the key to your climb out of depression.

I've filled in the chart in a different font so that you can see how to use it.

Date: *14 September*   **Time:** *3:30 p.m.*
What is it that I have to do?
Go out for a meal.
How much do I want to do it? (In percentage)
Minus 300%!!
What am I telling myself about this event? (Negative thinking)
I hate going out in the evening.
I hate eating late.
If I have to sit next to a man and he is a noisy eater, I might freak out.
It will be boring. I will have to make polite conversation. I'm hopeless at that.

People will dislike me; I'm such an awful person.
I might get "high" and end up hating myself.

Later
Date: *Same day*   **Time:** *10:50 p.m.*
How well did I cope with it/enjoy it?
Did quite well.
The food was delicious.
Chocolate pudding was great.
Nothing too crunchy, so I didn't freak out.
What is my percentage of enjoyment or success at coping with it?
90%
Looking back at my negative thinking, what can I challenge myself to confront?
I thought everyone would hate me, but they didn't.
People were really friendly.
I don't know why I assumed it would be boring.
I met some interesting people.
What did I learn?
It wasn't nearly as bad as I expected, and that keeps happening.

When we look back at our negative thinking and challenge ourselves to find other ways of seeing a particular situation, we can see how wrong we can be in our assumptions and our understandings.

- Just because I didn't get that task right the first time doesn't mean that I am totally hopeless at my job. I just didn't get that bit right today.
- Just because he didn't smile at me today doesn't mean he's gone off me forever.
- I totally fell apart today after being criticized. Okay, I'm really bad at taking criticism: It feels like the world has come to an end and I don't deserve a place on God's earth. But I can get better at handling it if I work at it by using the chart.

If we really commit ourselves to analyzing what drags us down we can change, over months and years, the guilt, fear, confusion, anger, worthlessness, and despair we tend to feel during depression.

I also learned as I did the charts that I tended to engage in a hopeless "if only it were different" kind of thinking. I had to see that the charts could help me change how I perceived the world and that this was going to help me much more than pathetically bleating "If only . . ."

Playing old familiar tapes

The things that we habitually tell ourselves are "old tapes" that we play to ourselves. They are the result of things that happened to us years ago. These relics of the past may stem from childhood, when we had just a child's limited view of the world and, inevitably, got things wrong.

So maybe we perceived ourselves as useless, worthless, unlovable. A child, unable to understand the world around her, concludes that adults are "good" and "right" because that is what children are taught to think. Therefore, if an adult treats her badly, puts her down, or is constantly criticizing her, the child assumes it is she who is "bad." These views of ourselves and the world go on playing over and over again in our minds. They become a part of our innermost being.

We tell ourselves we are no good. This is an old tape. It is the beginning of low self-esteem and a common root cause of our finding ourselves at the foot of the cliff. We need to—and we can—exchange those "old tapes" for new ones that are more accurate and more positive.

Emotions change slowly

Before you begin working on your "old tapes," it is crucial that you understand that we can be very logical about something, we can understand it, we can even change our beliefs ("I'm not useless, I'm an okay person"), but our emotions tell us differently. Emotions change slowly. When our mind tells us it's okay, our emotions yell out, "No it isn't."

We need to go on working at those "old tapes" until our emotions follow. That's hard work.

Come to me, all you who are weary and burdened, and I will give you rest. Take my yoke upon you and learn from

me, for I am gentle and humble in heart, and you will
find rest for your souls. For my yoke is easy and my
burden is light.
—*Jesus, in the Gospel of Matthew*

What am I saying to myself?

**Our self-esteem and our ability to love ourselves and
others in the right way rests on the fact that God loves
us. Each person is unique and infinitely valuable to Him.**
—*Dr. Richard Winter*

One of the most useful things that I have learned to do in the last few
years is to identify what it is that I am telling myself. Most of us have
this "negative self-talk."

This way of dealing with our problems (identifying our negative
thinking) is the basis of "cognitive therapy."

As we go about our ordinary lives, these "old tapes," stuck in our
minds and repeatedly blaring out at us, tell us such things as:

I'll always fail at everything that I do.

Everything is against me.

I'm always . . .

*Because . . . happened to me when I was five, I can never get away
    from it.*

I am utterly alone now and always will be.

God doesn't love me.

No one loves me.

I am of no value.

These "old tapes" are, for many of us, one of the root causes of our
depression.

Okay, your hormones got out of balance at the birth of the baby. Yes,
the death was hard to cope with and was the trigger for it all. Yes,
menopause is hell. Yes, being unemployed is terrible. Yes, looking after
Dad for all those years drove you crazy.

But it is the old tapes from long ago and from those recent
horrendous experiences that keep the icy fingers of depression around

our innermost being. Crucial to our successful climb out of depression is the identification of what is on these old tapes: our negative self-talk.

The ten commandments of self-defeat

Some years ago a friend of mine showed me these "ten commandments," which were written by Richard L. Mason. They are funny but sum up the most profound and difficult-to-identify beliefs that we have about ourselves and about our world.

And the devil said unto his angels, "Wreak havoc on the earth. Create unhappiness everywhere. Sow fear, worry, anger and depression in Jerusalem, in Judea and to the uttermost parts of the earth. For as I go, so send I you."

And one of the angels, whose name was Blame, settled on the fertile valleys along the Ohio River. There he began to teach the ten commandments:

1. Thou shalt never make mistakes.
2. Thou shalt upset thyself when things go wrong.
3. Thou shalt blame thy neighbour as thyself.
4. Thou shalt neither love, nor forgive, nor accept thyself.
5. Thou shalt always expect things to be different from the way they are.
6. Thou shalt seek the love and approval of everyone for everything that thou doest.
7. Thou shalt avoid facing life's difficulties, remembering that thou canst not change because thou art trapped by thy past.
8. Thou shalt be preoccupied with whatever bothers thee.
9. Thou shalt wait passively for happiness to come unto thee.
10. Thou shalt be dependent mostly on others for thy happiness.

And as Blame taught the people of the valleys, they believed him. In great numbers they came, and heard

and believed, so that the earth was truly filled with fear, worry, anger and depression.

Think

- Read through the "ten commandments" slowly and carefully. Jot down things that come to mind. Try to talk to someone about what you are thinking.

Activity

- Proceed with using the negative-thinking chart. If you are finding it hard to get going, try to identify just one negative thought on the first day.

When we are used to the chart, the sorts of things that we find out about our way of thinking about ourselves might be:

"I'm no good. I do everything wrong."—When a situation starts to go wrong we blame ourselves automatically.

"They hate me." "No one appreciates me." "Our marriage is falling apart."—When someone fails to give us the affirmation we thought we needed and deserved ("What a totally wonderful pie that was").

"I might just as well be dead."—When we feel we cannot possibly get up and go to work. It proves that we are useless, that life will always be this bad.

Why did that hurt so much?

We can make further use of the negative-thinking chart when we have used it a few times. We can start to "challenge" or analyze our thinking. (This idea is from David Burns's book *Feeling Good: The New Mood Therapy.*)

Beware! Doing this activity can be fairly terrible! I've written out one example from one of the charts I did a few years ago, and the note at the end of it says, "This was hell to write." It was such hell that I remember vividly, even now, the trauma of trying to work through it.

Do this on a day when you are feeling strong!

1. *Take one negative thought from a negative-thinking chart you have done.* For example, on one of the charts that I did after a meeting in which my boss repeatedly criticized me in front of my colleagues, I wrote: "She [my boss] really hates me."
2. *Try to work out why that negative thought from the "old tapes" hurt so much.* I did this in a series of questions and answers, trying to answer the negative thought with a positive answer.
3. *Go on doing this until you can get to a basic underlying belief that you have about yourself.*

These basic underlying beliefs that we have about ourselves are important because they can include the things that are keeping us depressed. We need to find out what they are.

Getting someone else to help you to answer your negative thoughts with positive ones might be helpful.

Negative automatic thought: "She really hates me."

Positive answer: "So what? Other people love me."

I noted in my journal that my self-esteem, my worth as a person, was very bound up with other people valuing me. I had this underlying belief that I was only worthwhile if other people thought so. This was made much worse in a professional situation in which I was continually criticized. The exercise didn't make the criticism any easier to cope with, but I learned something about myself and about why I was finding it so stressful.

The exercise worked with most negative thoughts, some more easily than others. For some, however, I needed someone to work with me.

As I worked with these charts over the next few months another thing became clear: I only saw myself as a worthwhile person when I was working in a paid job. This explained a great deal about my lifestyle and about my view of myself.

Getting to these underlying beliefs about ourselves is a crucial survival strategy.

If you believe that you are bad and unacceptable you see your anger as evidence of your badness. Thus you cannot cope with your anger or anyone else's anger.
—*Dorothy Rowe*

Part 5
Hanging On

20

Getting to know ourselves

It is only when we possess ourselves that we can give ourselves to others, [but] if what we possess feels wrong, bad, or wicked, then we not only try to hide it from others, but we also try to hide it from ourselves.
—*Jack Dominian*

If we are ever to hang on and climb out of depression, one of the vital things we need to do is to get to know ourselves. We need to know our strengths and weaknesses, and what, inside us, makes us as we are.

We need to know how to pace our lives. If you're like me, you will have good days and bad days. Sometimes the bad days go on for weeks and months, but you *will* get more done on some days than on others.

On good days I know I can get lots of things done. I just have to be careful not to do too much, although it is tempting, because then I get exhausted. I try to make myself stop well before bedtime, take a shower and then relax.

If you have ever been given the label "manic depressive" (one of my own collection), then this pattern of overdoing it some days will be familiar to you. It's difficult to develop the skill for both "making hay while the sun shines" and yet not leaving yourself shattered for the next day. It's all a question of pacing yourself. To do that well you need to get to know what makes you tick.

I suppose that by being kind to ourselves we might be in danger of turning into the most terrible procrastinators, but I think that this is a danger we need to learn to live with.

Surviving the climb out of depression is not just one long (desperately long) climb. It goes in fits and starts. Quite a lot of stops too.

Sometimes we need to retreat

Giving up today and retreating to somewhere safe is not a "bad" thing to do. It is nothing to feel guilty about. Depressed people seem to suffer most dreadfully from guilt. Most of this guilt is totally inappropriate. We need to see it for what it is. It is making us worse! Giving up today might in the end be a productive and positive thing to do.

"Human becomings"

It is an extraordinarily difficult thing to get to know ourselves. I don't suppose that we ever totally achieve it. It will always be an ongoing process. As someone put it, we are "human becomings." We seem, like it or not, to be on a journey. It is an excruciating journey at times, and we often feel like throwing in the towel.

I have come to see life as a kind of pilgrimage. I'm very suspicious of those people who give out the message that they have "got there." They have arrived. My life never seems to be like that. The minute I think I might have arrived, some other great crisis looms and I realize I haven't. So now I just treat the whole of life as a journey.

"It will be better when . . ."

It is a great mistake to think that the problems that we are facing at the moment will one day go away and that life will be bliss from then on. Our present problems will one day go away but will be replaced by others. (Hopefully not quite as dreadful as depression!) That's just how life is.

The eighteen-year-old thinks life really begins when he leaves school. The young pregnant woman thinks that all will be well when she's reached her delivery date. The professional thinks that life will get better when she gets that promotion.

"It will be better when we get our new house . . ." "when I've got more money . . ." "when the old dear dies . . ." "when we get married . . ." "when the kids have left home . . ." "when . . ."

Of course some things would substantially change our lives for the better. The number of homeless people in the world at the moment is devastating. Today on the news I heard that a volcano in the Philippines erupted; thousands are homeless, and many are dead. There are some things that could make the lives of these people so much better that, as someone who has never been homeless, I can hardly understand.

It would be wrong to think that if a homeless family from the streets of my city were given a home tonight (and I wish they were), that all their problems would be over. Some of the very painful and immediate ones obviously would be, but, as the days went by, these problems might well be replaced by others: The children will get sick, Gran will die, and conception of the much longed-for new baby might never happen.

We often perpetuate a very odd view of real life as something that is trouble free, rather jolly, and loads of fun. I don't know anyone for whom life is like that, at least not for long. Life is hard.

There are times when the rich people I know seem to get bogged down by their money and worry so much about it that it seems better to be a bit short of cash! People who get to the top seem to have a life of stress. Those who want promotion will not be satisfied until they get it.

People who have no kids wish they did. Many of those who do have kids worry themselves sick about them. Married people develop a curious intolerance of their spouse. The number of divorces and separations among the people I know is alarmingly high. Some single people grieve and are lonely.

Everyone, just everyone, faces problems of one kind or another, and when one is solved, another replaces it. Life is like that. When we pat our children's heads and cuddle them saying "It'll be all right," perhaps we should balance that proper need for reassurance with some explanations of the realities of life.

Maybe we do our children no good by only telling them that life is "all right"? I'm not sure. The truth is that a great deal of the time it isn't all right. At least, it doesn't *feel* all right. But perhaps the world of the child needs to be a world of happy endings and reassurance. Certainly it cannot be right deliberately to give children a tough time because they need to learn that the world is a hard place.

Maybe what we need to do, and teach children to do, is to find a way not of pretending life is free from problems but of dealing with the problems creatively.

Think

- Do I expect too much of myself?
- Do I have unrealistic expectations of life?

21

Emotions are okay

Through violence you may murder the hater, but you do not murder the hate.
—*Martin Luther King, Jr.*

Emotions are okay. A bit scary at times, but they are okay. I don't see how they could ever be "wrong." They are part of us, the part we call our "heart and soul." They are part of the innermost and most vital part of our humanness. They are how I tell myself what I am thinking and feeling. They are unique and valuable.

Little-understood urges and emotions, pushed under the carpet and out of view, are still there. And if we refuse to acknowledge them they become like a deadly virus. Gradually they eat their way into our bodies, our minds, and then our innermost being, poisoning our whole existence unless we pull them out into the open and make some effort to deal with them.

We may feel that it would be harmful to let those emotions out, but I believe that it is just as harmful to bury them. In fact it is probably much *more* harmful. Buried emotions come out somehow, and when they do they affect us very deeply.

They can be devastating (we just have to look at the effects of our depression to see that). They are depressing because we cannot understand them, so they make us feel even less in control of our lives than we were. They make us fearful because we cannot understand them. For some of us this could be the root of panic attacks. We are actually afraid of ourselves.

They are frequently inappropriate as they force their way to the surface. So, we may experience furious rage when our child or partner does some small thing. The rage isn't about that small thing. The rage is about something quite different: a buried emotion lurking inside us.

Accepting what I'm really feeling

Accepting that I am angry may be one of the first steps in climbing out of depression. Accepting that I am hurt and damaged may be the first step in working out why I am so depressed. Accepting myself as a sexual being may be the first stage in reaching beyond my guilt to a place where I can say, with great joy, "Thank you, God, for giving me these wonderful feelings."

To say that we don't have feelings such as anger and sexual urges is both stupid and dangerous, but admitting that we do is also dangerous. We all know the kind of person who projects a calm persona but is a boiling and murderous rage just under the surface.

- It's dangerous to admit to feelings.
- It makes us vulnerable.
- It gets close to revealing that innermost bit of us that is us, our "heart and soul."

Getting "in touch" with our emotions

We go to great pains to protect and conceal the "unacceptable" part of ourselves that generates strong feelings. We hide it. For those of us who feel the abyss of depression, this hellhole is our defense against the even worse horrors of our true feelings, buried deep in our innermost selves.

One day, all the pent-up emotion will come bursting through our calm exterior like the steam in a boiler. If its exit is blocked up we will simply explode in a world-shattering and cataclysmic moment of destruction. That's what depression is: our attempt to contain that enormous driving energy boiling and churning around inside us.

The trouble with our buried emotions is that they pop out when we are not expecting them. At best this is utterly disconcerting, and at worst it can wreck our lives. We do hateful things to those who love us.

We cry when it is most inconvenient. We feel destructive anger when a shrug of exasperation would have been more appropriate.

The way out of this trap is to try to feel what we are feeling *at the moment*. That's dangerous, and it hurts.

What can I do to get in touch?

Surprisingly, just by doing something creative or active, we can begin to identify what it is that we are feeling: anger, sadness, terror, and so on.

Punching a cushion when we feel depressed can help us start to see what may be causing our depression. As we punch, so things come to mind. As we write in our journal, we begin to understand ourselves more; we hear what we are thinking. As we create a new window box for the spring flowers, we hear some of our sadness over the death of the winter.

So, as we begin to piece together our own story of why we are depressed, our feelings become clearer. Maybe the way the woman in the supermarket treated us yesterday made us feel put down. The hassle with the man who came to service the boiler and left it leaking gas really got to us. The worry about a teenager, an elderly parent, the job we lost or facing up to a death—they can all make us angry, or fearful, or hostile. Once we recognize what it is that we are feeling, there is some relief but also fear.

What now?

Rather like standing at the bottom of a long and difficult climb, beginning to see the extent of those buried feelings is utterly daunting. If we say, "Yes, I do feel angry/abandoned/unloved," we have no idea where it will end. It is a great unknown. It is the stuff of nightmares.

But to recognize a feeling that we did not know we had is one of our greatest achievements. We begin to get a clearer picture of what is behind our depression. Although this picture is the stuff of nightmares, it is also the very thing that we need in order to make some real difference in our lives, to help us hang on.

Why do I feel this way?

"Why did I get so angry when she said that?" "Why did I feel such murderous rage at such an apparently small incident?" "Why has that death left me so fearful three years later?" "Why?"

It is neither easy nor comfortable to answer these questions, but at least if I know that I am feeling *something*, I am on the first ledge of the climb; it puts me in touch with myself as a person.

When we know we feel something, we are one stage up from the very depths of depression, when things are so bad that we feel nothing.

At the foot of the cliff there is a kind of alienating numbness to life that wraps us in a silent cocoon, because to feel those things that put us there would be too painful. So we feel almost nothing.

Once we begin to feel the rage, or the devastation of having been abandoned, or the horror of believing that it would be better for everyone if we were dead . . . then and only then do we know we are getting in touch with those feelings, and we are on the first ledge up the climb. We have made a start on the long and difficult climb to understanding ourselves. That is definitely a Good Thing! But it is also very painful and requires our hard work to deal with it.

> **Anyone who feels that they're in some way plugged into a meaningful, cosmic system is given a greater psychological balance and stability as a result—whether or not they believe it contains a God-like figure at the control panels. And lots of people have this beneficial sense of being plugged into something bigger, even if they're not religious in the going-to-church-regularly sense.**
> —*Robin Skynner, psychiatrist*

More about **being kind to ourselves**, chapter 7; **anger**, chapter 23; **guilt**, chapter 24.

The following three chapters deal with **fear, anger,** and **guilt**.

22

Overcoming fear, worry, and panic

Excessive fear is always powerless.
—*Aeschylus*

Depression is often accompanied by a devastating fear. If we are going to be able to hang on in our struggle up the cliff face, we need to learn some strategies for dealing with this fear.

It is not like the fear of getting cancer, or of dying in a terrible road accident, or our baby will die so we have to check every five minutes that she is still breathing. The fear during depression is something else as well.

We can never adequately explain it. It is worse for some than others. It goes beyond total panic or the fear of imminent tragedy. It haunts our lives. It rarely goes away. It makes us feel that at each moment of our day we must fight for our very survival. This fight for survival can be so terrible that sometimes we give up, and death seems to be a rather inviting option. At least the fear would end.

Facing the fear

It is not always associated with a panic attack: when the heart pounds, we break out into a sweat, we think we may throw up, and there are a thousand angry elephants stampeding through our stomach. The fear is something that just stays in our minds. In the dead of night, when we wake, it is there, lurking, reminding us that we have almost given up hope of ever feeling any different. It is like walking on a cliff in the dark knowing that there's a precipice nearby and that any minute now we will plunge to our death.

Sometimes it is worse than others. Maybe these times give us a hint of what lies behind the fear. This is the sort of information we need to write down. When do I feel the fear most intensely? What does it put me in touch with?

For me, the fear seemed to be there all of the time. Then I began to see how it was linked with a quite irrational fear of talking to a therapist about my childhood. There were certain things that would make the fear unbearable, as if life and the universe as I knew it would all come to some cataclysmic end.

This realization gave me some clues, but I had a very effective mechanism that would shut off my thoughts whenever I tried to think of what the fear was actually about. I would get some thoughts, the fear would leap out at me, then I would pull down the blind on those thoughts and I could go no further. For months nothing could get me beyond that point.

Clearly it was sensible to leave the blinds down; to raise them would be to cause the end of the world! But I had to get beyond that point eventually and learn to acknowledge my fear so that I could do something about overcoming it.

The trap

The fear can easily become horribly entangled with guilt, and when it does we get the feeling that our depression is deserved. It is God punishing us. We are such terrible people that it is only just and right that we should be dealt with in this way.

We both fear death and long for it to remove us from the fear of this terrible life. It is obvious that, given the strength of our feeling, we contemplate suicide. But what if we consider the possibility that death brings something much worse than this awful existence? Maybe there is no way forward. Both death and life are equally intolerable. And so the depression tightens its grip on us. Hopelessness sets in. We start to believe that there is no way out of this trap.

> **I have of late—but wherefore I know not—lost all my mirth, foregone all custom of exercises; and indeed it goes so heavily with my disposition that this goodly frame, the earth, seems to me a sterile promontory.**
> —*Shakespeare,* Hamlet

Decisions

This fear can bring with it a complete inability to make decisions. Do I want an egg or a cheese sandwich? Shall I wear the blue sweater or the green one? (It is no wonder, given this inability to decide these simple things, that our families give up on us.)

There are probably many reasons for this inability to decide, but one is that the fear prevents me from believing in myself. Any decision I make is bound to be wrong because I'm so hopeless. I'm going to retreat under my quilt so that I will not have to make any decisions. All I need to do there is hide and survive long enough for the worst of it to pass.

The trouble with that is that others want to help, so they ask, "What can I do?" "Would you like a cup of tea?" "Shall I turn the television on?" All these questions require a decision! I don't know what to say. I'm terrified. If I decide anything, something terrible will happen to change my life forever. The whole universe will explode.

How do we survive the fear?

One way is to look back at our strategies for facing the really bad times (see chapters 12 and 13). They can remind us that it will not always be like this. The worst of the fear will pass. Okay, it does not go away completely, but at times it gets a little better, better enough for us to come out from under the quilt.

An even simpler way to survive is to take a tranquilizer. I'm trying not to do that very much these days, and when I do, I use substitutes for the hard stuff that doctors prescribe (which can be addictive) from health food shops. These are mild herbal tranquilizers, usually based on valerian, lettuce, or chamomile, all of which are not addictive. I find them very effective, and there is never a sense that you must have one in order to survive the next ten minutes as there is with some prescribed drugs. As a short-term relief for the bad times, it seems sensible to me to use what is available. Ingesting valerian, lettuce, or chamomile probably is less harmful than allowing our bodies to live in such a state of panic that adrenaline is pumped out into our bloodstream for most of our waking hours and our heart is beating overtime.

Herbal teas help too. I like the taste, they are soothing, and I have to do something in order to drink them. Sometimes just putting the kettle on can help me back into the ordinary world, where maybe there are not too many monsters out to destroy me.

Relaxation exercises are great. They change the rate at which the elephants gallop through my gut. The trouble with these relaxation exercises is that although they are simple, they do require some drive, concentration, and determination on our part to quell the fear. That can require a belief in ourselves that we don't always have.

In the end, the fear will pass—a bit—but to get rid of it on a long-term basis we need to understand it. Somehow (usually with the help of some trusted friend or therapist), we must take the fear apart, bit by bit, and look at it long enough to understand it.

It is a long process. I learned not to rush it! It needs time.

Overcoming worry: the deathbed test

We worry terribly about things, but worrying never solved anything or made it better, only worse. When we come up against the overhang on the cliff and it seems impossible to go on, the deathbed test is good.

We need to ask ourselves, "Will I worry about this on my deathbed?" Our immediate answer is "Yes." But if we think about it, we may find that the thing causing us so much stress is not something we will even remember at the end of our lives.

Some of the things we worry about now will, I suppose, be of great and lasting significance. But when we know that our end is near, what will we be thinking about? Probably not today's major hurdle.

I've used the deathbed test so much that I know it works. I've even fine-tuned it to "Will I worry about this tomorrow?" Sometimes, when I recognize that the great worry of today will be tiny tomorrow, I can even let it go today. Now.

This has been my most important achievement in recent years. Because I was able to change how I think about my worries, I have hope that things can get better.

Dealing with today's worries

• Keep busy.
• Make a list of things that need to be done.
• Set a time limit on worrying. This sounds incredibly stupid, but it works! I decide how long I will allow myself to worry about something: ten minutes, perhaps, over a cup of tea. When the time is up I make myself go and do

something that will get the worry back where it belongs: write a letter, make a phone call, or write down what it is that is getting to me. Then I make myself do something else.
- Give it the deathbed test.

Dealing with panic attacks

Our bodies go through such a lot when the adrenaline is pumping, telling us that it is all too much.

- Develop some way to turn all that stress into action. Punch a cushion, rip the phone directory (the old one) in half. This needs to be planned ahead, otherwise you tend to get carried away, which can possibly get expensive and dangerous for those around.
- Have some technique for relaxing during a panic attack. Make yourself do it when the panic strikes!

This is rather like the relaxation exercise in chapter 10, but it can be done in a crowd.
1. *Breathe deeply.*
2. *Tense muscles (not easy to do with people around, but do as much as possible, such as clench fists and tighten foot and leg muscles).*
3. *Consciously relax every muscle.*
4. *Keep breathing deeply, stay relaxed, and face the cause of the panic head on.*

- When there is no clue to what caused the panic, try to work out what was going on. Why did the panic come now? What is it that I am so afraid of? (I get surprising answers.)
- If strategies for dealing with panic aren't working for you at the moment, or if life is so terrible that taking the easiest way out is the only way out, then reach for the valerian! That's only a short-term solution, but it's okay for now.

Activity

- Write down what the fear feels like.
- When does it get worse? (It may take several weeks to get a clear picture of what might be the root of the fear.)
- What might the fear be about? (Take a guess. Sometimes our intuitive guesses can give us a clue. It doesn't matter if we are wrong at this early stage.)

One cloud is enough to eclipse all the sun.
—*Thomas Fuller*

23

Understanding our anger

It is easy to fly into a passion—anybody can do that—but to be angry with the right person to the right extent and at the right time and with the right object and in the right way—that is not easy, and it is not everyone who can do it.
—*Aristotle*

Getting angry is natural. It's like getting tired, or hungry, or wanting sex. Not a lot we can do about the basic emotion; it's how we handle it and deal with it that we can control. There is not a lot of point in feeling guilty about these basic emotions, especially as we seem to have so little control over them.

Coming to terms with our feelings of hurt and anger is an important part of learning to hang on during the climb. This is especially true if part of our depression is trying to hold down our anger. Once we begin to see what it is that we are really feeling, and what it is that is behind our depression, we are on the way up the climb.

I often scream and rage at God. I think if he is all omni-whatsit and powerful—like I learned in religious studies at school—then he can handle a temper tantrum from one person. I don't believe he is thinking "Good grief, that Sue is a pain in the neck." It is much more likely he is thinking that it is a Good Thing that I am at last recognizing the amount of anger that there is inside me that has been sitting there undealt with for so many years.

> **You have a right to be angry, but you mustn't turn the anger in on yourself because that only compounds the damage which has already been done. You must turn the anger outwards.**
> —*Susan Howatch*

If God knows everything about me, he knows that I was thinking angry things anyway. Better to have it out. If I am unimpressed by the way he seems to be organizing life, I tell him with a disapproving roar. When we watch the news on television and see babies dying for lack of food, I think it is understandable that we question God's general management of the universe.

We don't get much explanation for drought, famine, volcanic explosion, hurricane, and tidal wave. God can hardly be surprised that we get a little irritated at times and sometimes raise a clenched fist heavenward. I rather think that he might appreciate our honesty.

Of course, we get angry with *people* too. That's not quite as easy to deal with and not nearly as easy for me to write about!

Am I angry?
Often, the problem with anger is that we do not realize it is there. None of us likes the idea that we might be angry inside. It's very frightening, especially if the anger is so great that it might include murderous thoughts. People have told me that it is as bad to think murderous thoughts as it is to actually commit murder. Something tells me that that cannot possibly be true. For one, you have a dead body; the other, you don't. Quite different, especially for the potential corpse.

Controlled expressions of anger

I believe in the controlled expression of emotions because part of the reason for depression may be this submerged anger (or any other emotion). When I teach small children at school (quite the most challenging job in the whole universe), I encourage them to pound the big cushions in the reading corner and to tell me what it is that has made them angry. I reassure them that it is okay to feel that anger but not such a good idea to go and punch Harry! I suggest that maybe they want to go and run around the playground to work off that aggression.

> **Usually when people are sad, they don't do anything.
> They just cry over their condition. But when they get
> angry, they bring about a change.**
> —Malcolm X

I'm quite sure that there is no easy answer to understanding and getting rid of buried anger. But what has worked for me is trying to express the anger in ways that don't hurt anyone. These are ways I have found to be effective:

*Kicking a wall. (I once did it to drywall, and my foot
    went right through it! Check first.)*
*Making bread. All that punching and kneading of the dough is so
    therapeutic.*
Furiously digging the garden.
Playing some aggressive sport.
Going a long way away from everyone and screaming.
Running down the street.
Punching a big cushion very hard and repeatedly.
Dancing to very loud music.

When I write a letter to God in my journal, I definitely feel better. I'm sure if I didn't do that the anger would be directed at my partner or my children or at myself in some destructive act. I'm sure God can handle it, and I think that level of honesty with him is something to feel glad about.

Think

- Find a quiet corner and start a list of the things that make you angry. What were the things that made you angry as a child? What is it that you still resent and feel bitter about? Your list might read something like this:

  I hated the way my dad was always too busy to play with me.

  My mother always nagged me. She made me wear hideous clothes, and the other kids laughed at me.

  They both wanted me to achieve above anything else. I never felt I was good enough for them. If I didn't get straight A's I had failed them.

  They favored my brother more than me.

  I hated school.

- List the memories of childhood that still stand out for you. What is the earliest thing you can remember? What is the most frightening thing you have ever experienced? What makes you angry now?

- It is often said that depression is internalized anger. How could you get to find out what anger there may be inside you? You may decide to: ask a trusted friend if he or she thinks you are angry inside; keep a note of what makes you feel angry/anxious/depressed; keep a dream journal; assume that there is anger there, even though you cannot see it, and take up some contact sport, such as squash or racquetball, or garden furiously for twenty minutes, or scream at the moon and see if that makes any difference.

- Anger may also be revealed through creative endeavors. What could you do to be creative?

  Read a story.

  Draw or paint a scene from your childhood.

  Join an evening class in pottery.

  Paint a mural on the bathroom wall.

  Grow cabbages.

  Arrange some flowers in your favorite vase.

  Write a long-overdue letter.

We don't have to stay trapped by what has gone before. We can decide to break free. People need not feel that their life is out of their control. It isn't. Have a good scream at God; he can take it!

24
Managing guilt

**Guilt always hurries towards its complement,
punishment: only there does its satisfaction lie.**
—*Lawrence Durrell*

There is a strong belief in Western society that there is a great deal to
feel guilty about. If we have really wronged someone then we should
feel guilty. It prompts us to do something about apologizing and trying
to put things right. But guilt seems also to surround the basic human
emotions that everyone feels. To have guilt about our sexual feelings or
our anger seems about as logical as having guilt about being thirsty.
It's human to have strong sexual feelings and to feel furious rage, and
it's okay to be human.

We can *feel* guilty without actually *being* guilty, and we can be guilty
without feeling it.

It's not wrong to feel angry, but it is wrong to kick the dog or to
murder the person we feel angry with. It's not wrong to feel very
sexually turned on, but it is wrong to rush out and leap into bed with
the first person we meet. It's not the emotion that is wrong; it's how
we deal with that emotion.

The kind of teaching that I received as a child and teenager seemed
to produce guilt in large doses. For many of us the guilt and frustration
and the sheer ignorance of our human urges has left us emotionally
paralyzed. Perhaps this is why so many of us try to bury our feelings.
If they are submerged and we cannot see them, we argue, then we can
control them. But that's not the case.

Burying our true guilt so that we cannot see it is a bit like trying to
bury an angry lion in a child's sandbox. We can't bury it deep enough
to get rid of it, so it remains a potential source of harm. The guilt will
burst through as depression, rage, or violence. It would be simpler to
deal with the guilt as guilt by apologizing and asking for forgiveness,
agonizingly difficult though that be.

The best way to get rid of false guilt is by recognizing that it is misplaced. I'm sure that zealous parents and teachers—me included—have a lot to answer for.

The depressed person can feel guilty because she thinks she is expected to be some kind of superhuman being. This guilt and the failure to live up to our own high standards can kill.

This morning our local paper printed a heartrending story of a woman who killed her two children and then herself. As the whole village met in the church to light candles and pray, they wept without exception as they mourned for this woman, whom they described as a perfect mother with delightful children.

The story goes on, becoming more and more inexplicable with reports on the loving husband, the busy community life of the family, and the respect that they had in the village. Then at the end there are a few telltale lines as her father-in-law explains that she had been depressed lately and felt she had failed as a mother.

Guilt is deadly stuff. True guilt can be removed through acknowledgment and forgiveness. False guilt needs to be shown for what it is.

Prayer is not asking. It is a longing of the soul.
—*Mahatma Gandhi*

25

Understanding how we see ourselves: our self-esteem

The recurring theme predisposing [people] to depression is rejection and lack of self-esteem.
—*Dr. Richard Winter*

There are products in the shops in my town to make us thinner, fatter, fitter; to make our hair darker, lighter, stronger, curlier, less gray; to make our cheeks redder, nails longer, legs smoother. Products to hide skin blemishes, get rid of wrinkles, and reduce cellulite. Shoes that make us seem taller. Clothes to make us look slimmer. Whatever part of ourselves we dislike or want to change, someone will have a product for us.

This cannot but increase our dislike of ourselves. "I'm not good enough as I am." "Without this or that, I will not be acceptable." "I must keep myself up to date." "I must do what the rest of the crowd does." "I must hide my real self." "I must keep up appearances."

These products are not wrong in themselves. There is nothing wrong in having clean and shining hair or perfume that lifts the spirits (provided that no animal has suffered in its manufacture). But it is something of a condemnation that in Western societies there is often more spent on cosmetics in a year than on overseas aid.

"What would you like to change about yourself?"
  "Oh, hair, eyes, nose shape, lips, skin colour—oh, everything."
  —*Interviewer and female interviewee on BBC Television*

- Am I really only acceptable at the party if I wear makeup or smart, new, trendy clothes?
- Am I being taken in if I believe that I am only "cool" if I wear a certain color this year, if I prefer a particular kind of drink, if I drive the latest model of car, if I vacation in the "right" places?
- Is my life really better because I have an electric carving knife/power drill/blender/Plasma TV/the right kind of jeans? Or is it that I believe these things will make me feel more of a person? more as if I belong? more acceptable?

We pick up messages from our society that tell us we are not good enough. Some of us pick up similar things from our childhood. Teachers, parents, brothers, and sisters tell us we are no good. We do not measure up to their standard. We are ugly. Unwanted. Stupid. This is the sort of thing that we grow to believe about ourselves. The result is our low self-esteem: We do not really love ourselves. This lack of self-love leads to depression and needs to be examined more closely.

26

Boosting our self-esteem

I'm constantly surprised at the extraordinarily beneficial effect that meditation has.
—*John Cleese*

In my late teenage years, when the truth that life can be terrible was gradually dawning, I started learning about Christianity. Life was unbearable without any religion. Would it be any better with it?

I went to one of those very "hearty" churches. Do you know what I mean? Going to them is like eating that very knobbly kind of muesli that health food shops sell. As you gnaw and chew your way through it, it is such hard work that it is only the thought that it must be doing you some good that keeps you going.

This church was like that. I knew it was doing me some good—if only by virtue of kind and friendly people there—but it was really hard work to swallow.

It seemed to specialize in what I called the "worm stuff." The minister was particularly fond of telling us that we should all believe that "I am a worm and no man."

Utterly evil?

On quizzing the minister one day I discovered that being a "worm" was about being sinful. *Hmm.* That made it as clear as mud. Further enlightenment came one day when he talked to the youth club about "total depravity." We are, he told us, naturally and utterly evil.

Well, after about a year of this mind-boggling stuff I could make some sense of it. Having picked up clear messages that I was unwanted, unloved, useless, in the way, ugly, and a pain in the neck since the cradle, this "worm" stuff all fitted in very neatly.

The sense that I was making of the world was that I had got it right: I was evil, wicked, guilty, and unloved. The "religious" message made my depression worse!

Many depressed people can trace their feelings of utter worthlessness back to these kinds of messages that they picked up as children and young adults.

In most of my [school] lessons I felt worthless and stupid.
—*Sue Townsend*

At eighteen I thought I had sussed out life. But whatever I did, I was always left with a sense of utter hopelessness. The feelings of depression were clearly all that I deserved. I learned to say "God be merciful to me, a sinner," but I never got any further. I sifted everything that I saw in the world through my "worm-stuff sieve." The minister at the hearty church probably did say other more hopeful things, but I never received them.

Say something righteous and hopeful for a change.
—*Oddball in the film* Kelly's Heroes

I see now that my schoolteachers, whom I was so fond of, were trying to tell me different things, but I sifted out all the things that didn't fit with my view that I was a hopeless and useless person. It took many years for the "worm sieve" to stop operating. (I think it sometimes still operates even now.) I could only receive messages of my own worthlessness.

There are many things that can make people think that they are of little value:

Lack of attention from parents.

Position in the family: "As the oldest I always got the blame." "As the youngest I could never do what the others could."

Abuse, both physical and emotional, from a family member or close friend.

Unsettled childhood: constant moving or no close relationships.

Anything interpreted as rejection: "I wasn't worth loving."

Absence of praise and affirmation in childhood.

Changing my self-esteem

Changing how we view ourselves is difficult! Extremely difficult. The first step is recognizing the problem; many people who are depressed do not realize they have a low opinion of themselves, and the power that the thinking has in their lives. Once we recognize the way we view ourselves (and that's not easy) we are on our way.

The problem then is that if I think that I'm a hopeless, useless, ugly, unwanted person, I am on one side of the rock face. Books by earnest psychologists and psychiatrists tell us that if only we were over on the other side (by believing in ourselves, making the most of ourselves, accepting our great value, and so on) we would feel better and our depression would go away.

Hmm.

I can remember reading David Burns's book *Feeling Good* on a beautiful Mediterranean beach one year. It explains that I need to be over there on the other side of the rock face. It has stories of people realizing their need to change their view of themselves, changing it, then leaving Burns's consulting rooms free from their depression.

It all sounded a bit unlikely to me. It made me feel even more depressed. ("Other people can just walk away from their depression, but I can't because I'm such a hopeless person.")

What it didn't tell me was how I could get from one side to the other.

How can I change my view of myself?

I remember, as I read the David Burns book, feeling incredibly irritated and cross with the whole world. I never finished reading it! It was as if I had struggled up the rock face to a point where someone was now telling me that, in order to complete the rest of the climb, I needed to be on the other side of a wide chasm. The other side is beyond reach. There is no bridge. There is no one who can help me across. There are no ropes. I just cling on to one side, knowing that I have to get across.

If I believe that I am hopeless and useless, how can I possibly change that? It's true! I am hopeless and useless. To believe otherwise is just wrong. How can anyone change what they have believed about themselves since they were born?

Hang on. Did I believe that I was hopeless and useless when I was born? Babies don't think like that, do they? Isn't it more like "I'm hungry. You have the milk. Come here and let's get on with it—now"?

You are a beautiful human person.
—*Pip Wilson, youth worker*

How do we change from one side to the other?
Someone recently gave me a very helpful way of seeing the ways we view ourselves. These are the three S's. (The idea is from the work of Lawrence Crabb.) They are what we need to replace our old views of our worthlessness. We need to develop them in ourselves to get from one side of the rock face to the other. They are:
security
significance
self-worth.

Depression is about a lack of the three S's. If I feel
insecure
insignificant
worthless
then depression is probably inevitable.

The three S's are things to work on in creative ways: writing, gardening, making things for the house, and so on. It is a slow and painful process, but with our creativity, and relationships with others, we discover that we are of value, of enormous value. The only things that seemed to be able to penetrate the worm sieve and the brick wall I had built around myself were the people who loved me and were prepared to sit beside me and hold my hand.

• Advice is no good.
• Telling us to pull ourselves together is no good.
• All the activities in the world cannot replace a bit of tender loving care, some human warmth, and a hug.

Activities can tell us how we are thinking wrongly. They can show us what we need to do. They can show us something of the truth. They can enable us to encounter ourselves in fresh ways. But they can never take the place of love.

We can see love in the face of a little child, a kind gesture, the startling beauty of the Rocky Mountains, and the smile of a neighbor who reaches out to us in an act of simple practical friendship.

Factors in my own climb out of depression were the care of someone who listened to me, the care of others who would pray with me, and the care of a friend who sat beside me and held my hand. She would suggest that we do fun things, she prepared meals for me, and we laughed a lot. Looking back on it now, the most significant thing she did was just be my friend when I was finding the going tough.

With love one can live even without happiness.
—*Fyodor Dostoyevsky*

However much our Deeply Meaningful Something-or-others (the things we believe about our world and that tend to keep us depressed) have defined our world for us as a love-free zone, there *is* love out there. That's another of the Great Truths of life: Love does exist. We may not feel it this moment, but that is not evidence that it cannot be found.

Even when we have no human love, the fact is that God loves us. Without human love, however, it is virtually impossible to believe that there is any kind of love. Mostly, it seems, God tells us about his love through other people or things. For me, being able to see that there is love out there took many years.

A thought transfixed me: For the first time in my life I saw the truth as it is set into song by so many poets, proclaimed as the final wisdom by so many thinkers. The truth—that love is the ultimate and highest goal to which man can aspire. Then I grasped the meaning of the greatest secret that human poetry and human thought and belief have to impart: the salvation of man is through love and in love.
—*Victor Frankl,* Man's Search for Meaning

When we are at the foot of the cliff, we say "Rubbish," to all that. Transforming the view into the realization that we matter and are "beautiful human beings" may take years. Of course, I don't know exactly *how* we get from one side to the other! What I do know is that somehow I made that leap across.

I found that I started to believe in myself. I found that my self-esteem had changed. I began to believe that I was valued and loved.

I've worked with young people full-time now for twenty years, usually with kids who are seen as "delinquents" or "tough." The hard, tough image outside is a big front it seems to me; inside there is a sensitive, delicate human being who is hurting.
—*Pip Wilson*

Activity

- How well do the three S's apply to the way that you see yourself?
- Go back to the chart in chapter 19. When you have done a few of these charts, you will start to see some of the things that may be keeping you depressed. Here are some of the types of beliefs that you might find that you have:

I must do everything perfectly.
Everyone must make it clear that they approve of me all of the time.
I must prove myself to be a worthwhile person through the things I do.
Any criticism proves that I am no good at anything.
I am a worthwhile person only if it is clear to me that someone loves me.
The world must be a fair place, so this should not be happening to me.

It's changing this unrealistic type of thinking that will boost our self-esteem and help us to change from one set of beliefs about ourselves to another more positive one.

See the **"good enough" principle** in chapter 9.

27

Understanding the "losses" in our lives

I am free to change and grow.
—*David Augsburger*

Depression is almost always about some sort of loss. I don't mean losing an object, such as a precious piece of jewelry, although that is a devastating experience. I mean the loss of something that was part of us as a person.

You will know what I mean if you have ever been burgled. It's not what was taken so much as that strangers were there in your house. They went through your cupboards, even into the box where you keep your very special things. They stood in your room. They defiled it in some way that is deeply personal and yet very difficult to explain. Maybe it has something to do with the loss of privacy, of feeling secure, of feeling that we have a place that we have made our own and that expresses our personality. That someone stood there, uninvited, is traumatic. That is the sort of loss we experience in depression.

One helpful thing that we can do if we want to climb out of depression is to try to list these losses. I found that a very hard thing to do. But having made a list, over months, I found that their power began to diminish.

It shows again that once we can identify the sources of our depression, we can start to understand in order to overcome them.

My tears have been my food day and night.
—*The Psalmist*

In his book *Feeling Free*, Archibald Hart outlines four senses of "loss" and suggests that it is helpful to try to identify what is affecting us in order to understand our losses and come to terms with them.

- Real loss—This is a real and tangible loss of something physical:
  Death of a loved one
  Separation from someone you love
  *Loss of an object of great personal value such as a family heirloom,
  a treasured photograph, or an address book or diary*
  Moving from a house you love

- Abstract loss—This loss is not about actual objects but more about our
  personal life:
  Loss of love in a separation or from being jilted
  Loss of self-esteem from heavy criticism
  *Loss of self-esteem and ambition from being rejected for promotion
  or a substantial failure*
  *Loss of being needed when children leave home and the nest is
  empty*
  Loss of routine, and perhaps meaning, after retirement

In my experience, because these abstract losses are not immediately obvious, they can be incredibly powerful. We should make every effort to identify them. Once I had identified my lack of self-esteem I was able to do something about it. Unidentified, it was a drain on everything I did.

- Imagined loss—This type of loss is very powerful as it is difficult to identify.
  They are the losses we brood on in our mind, and are deeply embedded in
  our paranoid thoughts:
  *"There you are, I failed again. Doesn't that just prove that I'm no
  good?"*
  "No one loves me."
  "Everyone is against me."
  "I will always fail."
  "Everyone would be better off if I were dead."
  "I'm stuck with life as it is, and I can do nothing to change it."

This type of thinking is at the heart of powerful psychological factors in depression. It is "negative thinking" that we must learn to counteract by testing and checking. (Just because she didn't smile at me doesn't mean she hates me.) We start to grasp what these imagined losses are when we are prepared to listen to the pain. What is it telling me?

I found that imagined losses were dominating my mind. It was incredibly difficult to identify and counteract those thoughts, but learning to do so has been one of the main ways I have been able to hang on.

• Threatened loss—Hart's fourth category is the fear of the future, living with the worry about what may happen:
  Death of a partner or a child
  Loss of a job
  Loss of your home, reputation, career, health, and so on

These potential losses can be much more powerful than the actual loss would be. If my partner dies when I am thirty, I might be more or less able to cope without him by the time I am thirty-five. But if, when I'm thirty, I live with the fear of his impending death, it will still be severely debilitating when I'm fifty and beyond, though he may still be alive.

We need to look carefully at our worries to see if we can free ourselves from the threat of loss that we are living under.

Activity

• Try to list your losses. Use the four headings in this chapter to help find as many of the losses as possible.

I've always been struck by the way so many patients, if they do well in therapy, develop an interest in the meaning and purpose of life.
—*Robin Skynner, psychiatrist*

28

Understanding stresses

Over-much stress or un-managed stress can bring a lot of trouble, but we can't do without it altogether. Stress is vitalizing, necessary, often enjoyable and constructive; if we look at it straight, we can learn to come to terms with both its effects and its management.
—*Wanda Nash*

It is probably fairly obvious that some of the things that happen to us during our climb through life are stressful. In turn this stress can lead to depression. It all gets to be too much, and so our bodies give in.

If you got married, moved to a new town, started a new job, tried to make new friends but desperately missed your old ones, took out a large loan to buy a new house, then found that your new job didn't suit you, it would be a bit surprising if you didn't feel overwhelmed.

One big event, such as a bereavement, can give us the creeping sensation of being cut off from everything, alone and afraid.

Something else may seem trivial but worries us deeply. We dare not admit how much it gets to us. We feel ashamed and guilty. Some people call these things that cause us stress "life events."

Life events

There are various charts of "life events" that list things that may cause us stress. The list below is an adaptation of the chart by psychiatrists Thomas Holmes and Richard Rahe. It starts with the life events that will probably cause the most stress. But remember that everyone is different. What one person may find insignificant another person may perceive as traumatic.

The idea of the list is to show us that if we experience more than one major life event (the ones near the top of the list) in a year, distress of some kind is very likely to follow.

However, although some of the items nearer the bottom of the list look uncomplicated, under certain circumstances they can be the last straw. Things were bad enough as it was, we were just coping, but the thought of having to get ready and face Christmas is just the end! We want to cancel it this year. We feel the guilt starting. We are embarrassed by our feelings.

The fact is that any kind of change at all can cause us to feel disoriented, even if we perceive the change as a good thing, such as a reconciliation or a great holiday. In this list the ones that are the most likely to cause the most stress are near the top. Two events from the top half of the list within twelve months could spell trouble.

Death of partner
Divorce
Moving house
Separation from partner
Jail sentence
Death of a close family member
Illness or injury
Marriage
Loss of job
Reconciliation with partner
Retirement
Health problem of close family member
Pregnancy
Sex problems
Major change at work
Change of financial status
Death of a close friend
Change in type of work
Increase in marital arguments
Taking out a large mortgage
Changes in responsibilities at work
Departure of child from home
In-law problems
Realization of a major achievement

Partner's starting or stopping work
Starting or leaving school or college
Change in living conditions
Change in personal habits
Difficulties with employer
Change in working hours
Change in place of residence
Change in school or college
Change in recreational habits
Change in church or social activities
Measures to take out small loan
Change in sleeping habits
Change in family get-togethers
Change in eating habits
Holiday
Christmas
Minor violation of the law

Individual reactions to things on the list will vary enormously. For example, if Christmas was always terrible when you were a child, when the first decorations go up (in August it seems sometimes), you get nagging anxiety in the pit of your stomach. If Christmas was terrific in the past but now you are on your own, that same feeling of pain will be there. So Christmas might be nearer the top of some people's personal life events list than it will be on others'.

The point about the list is that it can alert us to the realities of our life at the moment. Depression will not inevitably follow, but signs of distress will be there, and we need to recognize, think about, and listen to them so that we can make adjustments (planning more rest, for example). If your life has been stressful, you need to be realistic. You will recover from things much more quickly if you learn to be kind to yourself.

When I recognize that in the last few months I have had more than my fair share of life events, I can fight hard to stop the stress from pulling me down into depression. It is when we don't see or admit to stress that we are in for trouble.

Equally to be avoided is the sense that, as you have had three major life events in the last year, you should be allowed to be depressed!

Things may be easier if you talk them through with your family: "Look, I'm sorry that at times I'm unreasonable. Things have all been a bit much lately, and I'm struggling a bit. I'll try to cope with it."

What isn't so good is the utterly selfish bad-tempered behavior that expects the world to work around us and our problems. I know I have been like that at times! There is something about depression that does make us self-centered and self-protective (we need to survive). At times that is a good thing.

But there is a great difference between deciding some things about our own lives that we want to be different (such as our domestic or work role) and selfish behavior that insists that we are the center of the universe. We must struggle to see when we are like that and to stop ourselves.

Think

- Assess your own life events in the past year or two. (Some things not on the list may have affected you deeply.)
- Write down some of the things you can control and change, such as what you do, or think, or how you choose to react to things.
- Write down other things you cannot control and change, such as a death or a lost job. Some depression may arise because we are trying to change or refusing to accept things that we have absolutely no control over.

Activity

An important skill in dealing with stress is to make a list of what needs to be done:

- Put things in order of priority; what you need to do today and what could wait until tomorrow.
- Set goals.
- Do what you can today rather than worrying about all that needs to be done.

Lord, grant me the serenity to accept the things I cannot change, courage to change the things I can, and wisdom to know the difference.
—*Reinhold Niebuhr, theologian*

29

Fears

God weeps with us so that we may one day laugh with him.
—*Jürgen Moltmann, theologian*

Carrying on "normal" life is a big pressure for a depressed person. It is desperately embarrassing to have to say that you cannot come tonight or go to work this week, because you are depressed. Often people simply do not understand.

Some of my more extroverted friends who are depressed think that this aspect is slightly easier for them. They derive their energy from being with others, so meeting people may actually make them feel better. For those of us who are more introverted (those who survive and thrive by having time on their own), social life is a continual torment.

I never really resolved how to deal with this during the very bad patches. I didn't want to have to talk to anyone except my immediate family all day (and I needed long breaks from them). I didn't want to go to the shop to get the quart of milk. I didn't want to go out to friends who had invited us over. I didn't want to go to work. I certainly didn't want to go anywhere where there would be noise and where I would be surrrounded by people.

Naturally enough, my apparent unfriendliness and unsociability was misunderstood. This is just one of the many trials of being depressed, and there really is very little that you can do about it. We can try to explain to good and sensitive friends, but we run a great risk if we open our mouths at all.

Coping with phobias

Trying to get over the sorts of phobias that often accompany depression is hard work. Often others lack understanding, and we may be able to see how totally irrational it is, which makes us feel we are "being silly." Our self-esteem takes quite a knock. If I can't cope with taking the baby in the stroller down to the supermarket, I must be going mad! What do I fear will happen if I go out of the door?

Here are some of the fears that complicate our lives:

certain places

crowds

heights or enclosed spaces

certain circumstances: being sick, coming face-to-face with a spider, or being in a room where people are eating

being abandoned and left alone

sex

There are many more. The phobia can be about anything, from the baby's crib to ATMs.

What is a phobia?

A phobia is an irrational fear. It's like having a panic attack, but it is always about a particular thing that we can identify (unlike a panic attack, whose cause we often do not consciously know). The symptoms are the same: overwhelming feelings of terror, loss of control, nausea, trembling, dizziness, breathlessness, palpitations, sweaty palms, a need to go to the toilet, and shakiness or weakness in the limbs.

> **Phobias cut across class, education, and income, and most fears—with the exception of animal phobias—tend to rear their head in young-adult life. They strike women more than men and are more common among sensitive or highly intelligent individuals.**
> —*From a leaflet supplied by Depression Alliance*

Fear of things such as spiders or snakes is common, but so are these:

agoraphobia (a fear of open spaces or public places)

claustrophobia (a fear of being closed in)

social phobias (fears of social contact)

People often experience more than one phobia at a time. It is, for example, possible to be both agoraphobic and claustrophobic.

What causes the phobia?
Phobias vary so much that it is not easy to figure out what causes them. It's possible they are the result of some sort of traumatic event, such as a house move, or childbirth, or depression. Sometimes they can be attributed to things that happened in childhood.

What can I do?
1. *Ask for help.* Doctors and therapists seem to be able to deal quickly and effectively with phobias once they are told about them. We need not disguise them and say that we are "anxious." If we actually check twenty times that we shut the front door, or fear taking a train to the point where we become terrified, we would do well to pluck up the courage and say so. If we camouflage our phobia as "anxiety," the prescribed tranquilizers may not actually help us.
2. *Find out more information.* (See the resources at the end of the book.)
3. *Take courage from the fact that many people get over phobias completely.*
4. *Gradually learn to do the thing that you fear.* As a young mother, I found that I could just about cope with going out if I held on to the stroller. Without it I would panic, but with it I could gradually teach myself that I could get beyond the front door.

I still have to plan my life a bit around my fears, but facing them head-on is more effective than feeling that they are insurmountable barriers.

Valuing ourselves
We may feel that we are going crazy because of our fears and our thoughts. However, I'm told that when we worry that we are going mad, it is a sign that we probaby aren't. The really seriously mad people are not aware of their craziness. This may be only a small comfort, but it is at least some comfort.

Experiencing fears, phobias, suicidal thoughts, and irrational behavior during depression is not unusual. The fears will go away. One day we will feel significantly better. Nothing is gained and a great deal is lost by "blaming" ourselves and focusing on our uselessness and stupidity. We are valuable human beings.

Activity

- Make a list of positive things you can say about yourself or about the ways you are dealing with your fears and depression.

I'm trying to be kind to myself.

I'm going to get out of this depression one step at a time.

I'm good at my job.

I'm a "good enough" parent.

I've got some really great friends.

I'm working hard on the way I'm thinking and feeling . . . and I'm working at being patient!

I've got more realistic expectations of life now.

I've stopped giving myself unrealistic lists of things to do.

I recognize that crying is not being weak but a way of letting myself express what I am feeling.

Sometimes even to live is an act of courage.
—*Seneca*

Part 6
Falling Off

30
Falling off

Suicide is a very permanent solution to what is usually a temporary problem.
—*Dr. Richard Winter*

For most of us, life is a constant trial. Falling off is a frequent occurrence. Things get so bad that we are back at the foot of the cliff again. All the old feelings come back. We feel defeated, crushed, and disappointed. We think through our options. Death is one of them.

Tempted to jump off
Most people think about suicide at some stage in their life. Some make attempts at it. The trouble with thinking about it even once is that the thought comes back. At the first sign of trouble our mind immediately flips into "jumping-off mode." We become convinced that the world would be better without us. We don't think we can stand another minute.

Talking with friends who have had many suicidal thoughts, we all agree that it was our "illness" telling us that we would rather be dead. When we get better, we are overwhelmed with remorse at our thoughts, and so unbelievably grateful that we did not harm ourselves that it is almost too much to think about it.

Many suicide attempts are angry responses to difficult relationships or situations.
—*Dr. Richard Winter*

Those around us, who we assume would be glad to get us out of the way, would in fact be affected for the rest of their lives by our death.

Taking all the tablets prescribed by the doctor in one go is dangerous. It may well result in death but is more likely to end in irreparable brain damage. We wouldn't die; we would just become a cabbage.

Getting through the really unbearable patches

We need to be ready for these unbearable phases, when death seems quite a pleasant option. That's where our previously prepared collections of things for the really difficult times (see chapters 12 and 13) come in. Different people need to do different things. One of the following suggestions may help you:

- Don't make any big decisions while you are depressed. You would make different decisions if you were better.
- We simply cannot know what death is like. It might be the end of all our struggling, but, then again, it might not.
- Have a list of phone numbers for people you can call.
- If you don't feel you can phone people, go out somewhere. (I usually feel I'm unfit to be around people when it is really bad.) Do anything that will help time to pass so that the worst of the feeling diminishes a bit.
- Retreat to your "cave." Find somewhere where you can just "be," where no one will disturb you.
- Although it feels like the foot of the cliff again, it may be that you did not fall all the way down this time. What feels like the bottom may actually be a little further up each time. There is gradual progress.
- Cry, scream, write furiously, play very very loud music, kick the wall—anything that will channel the feelings of devastating and destructive depression into something other than the permanent self-destruction of suicide.
- If it is very early in the morning, I find that I just get more depressed if I stay in bed. Getting up and making a cup of tea improves things a bit.

If, in the end, you are really determined to kill yourself, there is not a lot anyone can do. But bear in mind the following:

- If you die there will almost certainly be people who will say, "I wish I had known how she felt. I would have liked to have helped." You may feel that no one will say that. That is probably more a sign of the illness than of reality.
- If you die, although you may not think so at the moment, some people would be desperately, desperately hurt. It would affect their lives forever. (If

that makes you think "Good, that will show them," try to work out if you really want to give up your life for such vengeance.)

- If you die it may well not be quite what you expect. We can't know that anything would be better than our living hell. You run the risk of failing to kill yourself and just permanently injuring yourself instead.
- Many suicidal feelings are a wish for more help. What we are really saying is much more "I cannot stand this hell," than "I want to be dead." Tell anyone who will listen and will talk it through with you. Ideally tell your doctor. My doctor is brilliant. If yours isn't, find a better one. It is very, very important to have a good doctor.

The desperate sadness of suicide

When someone cannot cope with depression any longer and a suicide is reported in the local paper, or in the magazine of the Depression Alliance, *A Single Step*, I wish I could have held that person's hand until the worst had passed. The sadness is overwhelming.

It is not just that someone was in such pain. Not just a sadness for the grieving family (and suicide must be the very hardest death to come to terms with), but a sadness that the person was alone in that pain.

THE GENERAL TREND IS UPWARD

CLIMBING UP

FALLING OFF

This aloneness at the depths of despair is the tragedy. We can feel that there is no one, but there are people out there who care and who can sit with us until we feel better. In the United States there are numerous confidential hotlines, or you can contact a local minister.

Sit it out. The hug that we need does exist; we just can't have it at the moment.

> **Trust not to thy feelings, for whatever they be now, they will quickly be changed towards some other thing.**
> —*Thomas à Kempis*

Do something "destructive!"

If this is making you angry—"How can she understand?"—maybe that's good. Some suicidal feelings are anger turned inward on ourselves. We become self-destructive. Recognizing and trying to express that internal anger is one step up.

It always makes me feel better to be "destructive" of something. Good choices, because the damage is only temporary, are lumps of clay in the garden, big cushions, and so on. Bad choices, because we may regret what we have done but cannot alter it, are kicking the dog, breaking something precious, or taking our own lives.

The issue here for our climb out of depression is that sometimes things need to be destroyed before they can be made better. The garden left undug will not give a good harvest. I once knocked down a wall in order to rebuild it. It was incredibly therapeutic, and out of the rubble came a new and pretty good wall.

> **May the road rise up to meet you,**
> **may the wind be always at your back,**
> **may the sun shine warm on your face,**
> **the rain fall softly on your fields;**
> **and until we meet again,**
> **may God hold you in the palm of his hand.**
> —*Celtic blessing*

Part 7
Making Progress

31

Picking ourselves up
and having another go

The only way to heal the pain that will not heal itself is to forgive the person who hurt you. Forgiving heals your memory as you change your memory's vision. When you release the wrongdoer from the wrong, you cut a malignant tumour out of your inner life. You set a prisoner free, but you discover that the real prisoner was yourself.
—*Lewis Smedes*

The good thing about restarting, even if it is from rock bottom, is that we know some of the possible ways up and some of the pitfalls. Not much else about restarting is good! We know that we have a long hard climb ahead of us. But we are not starting totally from scratch. It is a help that we already know where some of the handholds are.

We learned last time that it helps to be kind to ourselves, to eat sensibly, to exercise, to jot down the things that drive us crazy, to try to be a part of some self-help group, to keep adding to our store of coping strategies for the really bad days, and to do some of the things that we like doing. We are now a little wiser. We know that depression feels terrible. We know that some days are hell. We know not to make big decisions on the bad days.

Even those nearest to us (if we are lucky enough to have anyone close) are learning a bit about how to help us or at least how not to make it any worse! (Remember that helping us is almost impossible.)

Do I forgive myself and others?

**You will know no peace until you discover how to forgive
yourself, to forgive other people and to let others
forgive you.**
—*Dorothy Rowe*

Those who hang on to old hates and bitternesses and who refuse
to forgive or "let go" are people who become hateful and bitter
themselves. Those who are self-centered, bitter, and angry are a drag
to be with. Bitterness and resentment are ugly things; you can see
them in people's faces.

In great contrast, the old person whose face is alive with forgiveness,
love, and the wisdom of old age is a delight and a pleasure to be with.

No matter what has happened—how traumatic, unjust, unfair—we
will make the climb easier if we somehow unlock ourselves from it. We
must put it down, or we will be dragged down.

Forgive and forget?

It is not true that we must forgive and forget. Forgive, yes, but
forgetting seems unrealistic and at times nigh impossible. Some things
are so drastic that we are unlikely to forget them.

What "forgive and forget" means, I think, is that we forgive by
blotting something out and not holding it against someone anymore.
Forgiveness is a continuous thing; it doesn't happen once and for all.

As the years go by, the memories of wrongs people have done us
usually shrink if we have forgiven them. And we shouldn't strive to
remember. But forgiveness is also about remembering that it was that
bad and that we love the person so much that we still forgive them.
Lewis Smedes explores this point very helpfully in his book *Forgive
and Forget*:

**Forgetting, in fact, may be a dangerous way to escape
the inner surgery of the heart that we call forgiving.**

Saying "Sorry" and getting the immediate reply "That's all right,
it's all over and forgotten" is not necessarily the best thing.

Forgiveness is so much more than that. That immediate response is the most appropriate one for a small child who needs to be sure of our love and our acceptance, even when he or she is awful. But the real act of forgiveness is far too important to be rushed and delivered glibly.

Forgiving is difficult

Forgiving is one of the hardest things about the climb up out of depression. It's hard to forgive someone who is dead. It's especially hard to forgive if the hurt was the death itself. That hurts so much that you persistently feel rejected and abandoned.

It's hard to forgive people who aren't sorry or who are unaware of what they have done. Maybe they had the best of intentions, but it hurt you nonetheless. Parents and children know a lot about this. Most parents seem to make terrible mistakes with their children. Then children do likewise as they grow up!

It's hard to forgive when it is a part of an organization or a huge and anonymous system that wronged us. Losing our job or our home falls into this category. Health insurance companies may do terrible damage to someone who is depressed. There is nothing—or at least I can't think of anything—that we can profitably do about it, but somehow we need, for our own health's sake, to let it go and forgive.

It is hard to imagine, when a war ends, what pain and trauma the whole situation has caused. Most of the young military personnel come home, but they will never be the same as they were before. The families who try to cope without a loved one who didn't make it home will still be hurting for a generation.

Those who have been prisoners in a war will try to escape from their nightmares. People try to live alone in cardboard boxes. Shattered countries try to feed their hungry children. Others try to survive alongside each other in families. In each of those lives there is the desperate need for forgiveness. It will not come easily. Life is tough. As Paul S. Fiddes says:

Forgiveness is . . . a "shattering experience" for the one who forgives as well as for the one who is forgiven. This

is because forgiveness, unlike a mere pardon, seeks to
win the offender back into relationship. . ... Forgiveness
involves an acceptance which is costly.

How do I forgive someone?

Forgiving is difficult. I was wronged. It shouldn't have happened, but it
did. Nothing can change the event. What can change is the effect of the
event on me. The person who did wrong should be brought to justice,
but my forgiveness is to not demand this justice. I will go beyond that.
I will not stand on my rights; I will let it go.

Moving beyond ordinary human justice is the central core of
forgiveness. When we are able to do that "letting go," we say in effect
that we are not going to let the past dictate the future.

Of course it is incredibly hard to forgive. But when I consider the
way in which I believe God forgives and loves me, then I find I can
think of forgiving others. Mostly!

Not forgiving makes life even harder

Not to forgive will eventually cause our fingers to stiffen as we persist
in pointing accusingly at the one who caused us grief. Pointing,
accusing fingers cannot grip the rock. We will lose our handhold and
slip back two steps for every one that we take.

> **Vengeance is too little. Pardon is very much bigger and
> greater.**
> —*Irène Laure*

Our bodies will speak of bitterness and unresolved anger. We won't
be climbing for any reason other than to get back at those who have
injured us to prove them wrong, which is not a good reason for climbing.

The burden of it will slow us down, and should we reach the top, it
will have been such an excruciatingly dreadful climb that we will be
disillusioned and shattered. The summit will hold no joy, only another
reason to complain.

An act of will

Forgiveness is something that we can choose to do even if we do not "feel" able to do it perfectly. Forgiving is something that has a very definite start. That start is deciding that in the end we will forgive, even if at the moment we are:

- still feeling angry
- unsure of what we feel or of what really happened
- feeling anything but forgiving!

Maybe there is such a thing as "good enough" forgiveness. It's such a long and difficult process that for most of us, most of the time, we live with things inside us that we still need to let go and try to forgive.

It can be easier to see forgiveness more as "letting go": a long-term process we start because we do not want to turn into bitter, resentful people. "Letting go" can start with our:

- saying that we are not going to let "them" ruin our lives
- deciding we are "going to get beyond it" for the sake of our own mental health
- seeing that we can start a new phase of our life that will be much better than the old phase
- deciding to become creative and loving people
- being determined that any hurts we receive can be transformed into wisdom that will help us live lives better than those of people who abuse us

Pushed into forgiveness

There are always people eager to tell us that we "must forgive," while we are trying to work out what we are feeling. (One of the things that depressed people tell me about over and over again is the confusion they feel. If we don't know and understand what it is that we are feeling about something horrible that someone did to us, it is difficult to see how we can forgive them meaningfully.)

I've experienced this sense of being pushed into forgiving by people who seem to believe that "Forgive and forget" is the answer to everything. I've been told that God will forgive me only if I forgive my abusers. This is not true to my spiritual sense of God and the ways in which the world seems to work.

But don't forgive too soon

As I have struggled to free myself from the nightmares and phobias of having been abused as a child, I have had the privilege of sitting with other abuse survivors, trying to find out how we "let go" of our hurt.

For some people, the very thought of forgiving those who abused them is just too hard. Suppose their abuser, when confronted with what happened, just says

"So what? You deserved it."

"I will never apologize."

"That isn't abuse!'

"You need to apologize to me and to the rest of the family for saying all these things, and if you don't apologize, none of us ever wants to talk to you or see you ever again."

or goes on abusing? Then it is clearly such a hard task to forgive that we can feel defeated and hopeless.

Inevitably we ask, "Why should I forgive that person? What about justice?" What they did was wrong, and they are getting away with it.

- If we are pushed into forgiving too soon, our feelings are likely to be very unsettled.
- If we still feel angry and sad or feel that we "should" forgive but get horribly upset as soon as we hear the word "forgive," then we clearly still have things to work through. That will take time, and it is okay to take that time.
- It might be that the little child or young person who was so desperately hurt can't actually forgive the abuser—ever. As adults, however, we can decide to "let go" for the sake of our own mental health and forgive although the little child inside us may remain hurt.

There will be even more internal chaos if we rush into forgiving, perhaps even deceiving ourselves that we have already forgiven, and we say to those around us that "not one single thing about the past bothers us one tiny little bit now."

I know people who say that, and I find every one of them really scary. But it is a mistake to think that I know what is going on inside their heads. Of course, where they say they are is where we all want to be eventually: free from all the pain, free from depression, free to be ourselves.

Understanding forgiveness

As with many things, there is a time when it is right to forgive. We delay that time at great cost to our own well-being and our relationships with others. On the other hand, if we can see forgiveness as a long process, starting with our decision to "let go" for the sake of our own mental health, we are likely to be on a realistic path toward our own personal freedom from past hurts. Real forgiveness takes time.

Forgiving ourselves

Depressed people are usually bad at forgiving themselves. It is common for them to feel that because they are such terrible people they deserve to be depressed. It is a just and right punishment. An unbearable amount of guilt may be a sign that you are not forgiving yourself.

Putting down our burden of guilt

There is absolutely nothing that we can do that is too bad to be forgiven. There is no sexual sin, no wrong against someone we love (or hate), absolutely nothing in the whole universe that cannot be forgiven and the burden taken off our backs. If we hear a little voice telling us otherwise, is it some voice that we picked up along the way?

Many people who become depressed wonder if they have committed "the unforgivable sin." They may not know what this means, but they remember the phrase from Sunday school. I used to worry about it, but the best explanation of it, to me, is that it must have something to do with being so far against God that you insist evil is good. So, for example, people may argue that torture is "good." They have turned against God so far that they cannot see it is wrong.

Almost certainly, our worries about such sin are unfounded. Someone helpfully once said to me that anyone who is worried about having committed that sin is, by virtue of worrying about it, someone who hasn't committed it! So if you are worrying about having done some unforgivable wrong, it's a sure sign you haven't. If you are worried, ask a pastor from your local church for help.

> **Despair has been called the unforgivable sin—not presumably because God refuses to forgive it but because it despairs of the possibility of being forgiven.**
> —*Frederick Buechner*

Guilt is perhaps the hardest burden to put down. It clings to us like a bad smell, and we have to work hard to rid ourselves of it. It is far too heavy a burden for us to carry up the climb. When we are sorry (not an easy thing), when we have asked God for forgiveness, there is no place for guilt at all.

Even if humans can't or won't forgive us or aren't there to forgive us, God can and does. When we are sorry, the wrong has been wiped out. We can hold up our heads now. There is a place for sorrow but not for guilt.

If putting down the burden of guilt proves too difficult, get help. It isn't an easy thing to do. A friend or counselor may be able to help you unburden yourself.

The next stage

Once we are free from guilt we can race up the climb. But if you are like me, you will probably find that, after a while, the burdens are right back there weighing you down. We seem to get curiously attached to them. During unguarded moments we seem to rush back to hoist them back up.

Life has been depression, guilt, confusion, and so on for so long that we find it difficult to realize what a life of freedom might be like.

Maybe the very idea of life at the summit, beyond depression, is frightening. If I'm not depressed people will expect me to cope, to be okay, to get on with life. *Aargh!* I'm not ready for that. Depression is useful to me; I can hide behind it.

We need time. Time to cope with the idea of what life could be like. Time to let the gaping wounds heal. Time to work through the yelling and the tears. The habits we have learned over a lifetime are not easily left behind.

> **I have lost my daughter and we shall miss her. But I bear no ill will, I bear no grudge. Dirty sort of talk is not going to bring her back to life. Don't ask me please for a purpose. I don't have a purpose. I don't have an answer. But I know there has to be a plan. If I didn't think that I would commit suicide. It's part of a greater plan and God is good. And we shall meet again.**
> —Gordon Wilson, the father of a girl who was killed by a
> terrorist bomb at a Remembrance Day service in Enniskillen,
> Northern Ireland

32

Using our dreams to help us

We are not hypocrites in our dreams.
—William Hazlitt

Dreams are another part of our lives that can help us to make progress. When I first heard this suggestion during therapy, I thought it very silly, but I agreed to give it a try. To my surprise, it proved a valuable source of self-knowledge.

Dreams can help us find out what our Deeply Meaningful Something-or-others are: what is behind our depression, the cause of it. If we have pushed something down into our subconscious (which I take to mean that part of us that is unaware of what we might be really feeling or thinking), we have a potentially explosive situation. It may be that "listening" to our dreams could help us.

Important things often happen to children when they are so young that they are not able to express what they feel. These feelings are still inside us as adults, creating havoc. Buried, they are like a bottled-up boiler in which the steam is building up to a dangerous level. The pressure is so enormous that it could explode.

Our guard and defenses work hard in our waking hours to prevent all that grunge and muck from getting to the surface. When we are asleep they go off duty, so then it all tries to escape. It is trying to get messages to us.

- Please could you take some notice of me that when _____ died you were hurt?
- The reason you feel numb about _____ happening is you did not let yourself feel it.
- You were more deeply affected by _____ than you think.

Our bodies need us to *feel* that hurt and to recognize what it is so that we can start to deal with it.

I found a helpful book about dreams by Russ Parker. It was surprisingly easy to relate to my dreams on my own and to work out what my mind was trying to tell me. The really important thing that I found out was, as Russ Parker says, you must be ready to write down a few notes about your dreams, immediately upon waking. That's tedious, because it sometimes stops you from going back to sleep, which is a lot to cope with if your depression is causing you to sleep badly anyway. However, as with so many things about the climb, this short-term pain can lead to long-term benefits.

The best way to get myself to jot down details of the dream was to:

- have the pencil and paper ready by the bed
- have a low-wattage bulb in my bedside lamp (a bright light gave me such a shock that I instantly forgot the dream)
- write quickly
- never, never tell myself that I wouldn't need to write it down because I would remember it. If it is explosive stuff your consciousness wants to forget it, and it will

Then, in the morning, I would read my notes through, try to remember the dream, add extra bits that came to mind, rewrite bits that were illegible, and ask myself what it was that the dream was trying to tell me. You might find that this is something you can share with a trusted friend, if you have one, but I found that I was able to get a surprising amount from it myself.

> **O Lord, you have searched me**
>   **and you know me.**
> **You know when I sit and when I rise;**
>   **you perceive my thoughts from afar.**
> **You discern my going out and my lying down;**
>   **you are familiar with all my ways.**
> **Before a word is on my tongue**
>   **you know it completely O Lord.**
> **You hem me in—behind and before;**
>   **you have laid your hand upon me.**
> —*The Psalmist*

My dreams seemed to be a mixture of things that had recently happened, stuff so bizarre that I never knew what it could possibly be about, and old fears and nightmares that definitely rang bells once I got used to recognizing them.

For example, one dream was about me going up into the attic of our house (I had been up there the previous day looking for something). I refused to come down. My therapist was at the bottom of the ladder, telling me it was quite safe to come down, but I absolutely and vehemently refused, saying that it wasn't. I wanted to stay up there among the spiders and cobwebs.

It was pretty clear what that dream was about. I was holding my ground—depression and old patterns of thinking and behaving—and refusing to let anyone help me. I didn't want to change or move down into the light. I was alarmed to realize it was true. I *thought* I wanted to change, but I didn't really. I felt safer the way I was.

So dealing with dreams does come with a health warning: It is not easy, and, as with anything about depression, it can be painful.

Activity

- Put paper and pencil by your bed. (Make sure you have a hard enough surface to write on.)
- Change the bulb to a low-wattage one, or turn the light away from your eyes.
- Put some easy reading within reach if it helps you drift back to sleep after writing down your dream. Herbal tranquilizers too if you need them.

33

Loneliness

Loneliness causes greater suffering than cancer and leprosy.
—*Mother Teresa of Calcutta*

Sooner or later each one of us feels utterly alone on this strange little planet. People tell us it is not so. We try to believe that it is not so. We belong to clubs and societies. We write letters to our friends. We make dates in our diaries to meet them. We put up photos of our family. But all this conceals the truth that hits us in depression. When it comes to the crunch, we feel alone in a world of millions.

Loneliness is more about how we feel than about the experience of actually being on our own. Almost everyone knows that awful sensation of being with people and, at the same time, experiencing devastating loneliness.

Psychotherapy may be available to us. We may have a dozen close friends, a wonderful partner, but in the end each person has to work out her own way of understanding the world. I have to learn to fight my own battles within myself. I must decide for myself which direction to go in, whether to get to the top of the climb, to stay here on this ledge, or drop off. No one can climb for me. If someone tries to live his or her own life through me (parents are good at this) it will drive me to distraction and then into chaos and depression.

In solitude the lonely man is eaten up by himself.
—*Friedrich Nietzsche*

I am myself and only myself. No one sees the chaos and the ugliness of my mind or hears my silent cries for help. I'm there on the rock face, cold and alone. My fingers hurt. My arms and legs ache. My knees are trembling with the stress. I want to throw up.

This aloneness is the reality. Yet it is not the whole reality. It is only the reality of this moment. It is rather like the experience of winter. Spring will come, but it does not actually ease the gloom of the long, dark days. The hope of spring does not warm us up if we cannot afford to buy fuel. It is all very well to think of springtime ahead. Yes, it helps a bit, but the reality now is that it is dark and cold.

Life isn't just spring and new life. When we think of Jesus' death on the cross, the Resurrection was not the whole story. The bit in the grave must have hurt him. He went through hell.

Loneliness is bred of a mind that has grown earthbound. For the spirit has its homeland, which is the realm of the meaning of things.
—*Antoine de Saint-Exupéry*

Biology classes teach us that spring couldn't come without the depths of winter. We realize that we wouldn't enjoy the first flowers so much if they were with us for the whole year. Maybe we need the death and the gloom to understand and enjoy the spring.

Without physical death, the resurrection of Jesus would be nothing more than a walk in a garden on a spring morning. It would have no point. No power. To have resurrection you have to have had death. To know joy and peace, you have to have known turmoil and sorrow. Life without a struggle up the rock face would be a bland, boring walk in a flat, boring countryside. Featureless.

So the aloneness is not the end of the reality. Maybe reality has a time dimension too, and the end of the line will be both the suffering and the joy. The beginning and the end of the line may make up one unit, but we only experience one bit at a time.

Maybe reality is made up of both the death and the resurrection: winter and spring. It is both the isolation at my moment of crisis and also the comforting warmth of an understanding hug much later (sometimes very much later).

Not having that loving hug at the moment of my pain is a problem of time, not a problem of the truth of its existence. It is not true that at the moment of pain that hug does not exist. It just doesn't exist now.

There is the lifeline, and the leader holding on to that lifeline. But I am at one end, and the leader is at the other.

What is this loneliness?

There are many possible reasons why we feel so alone. Of all the symptoms of depression, the sense of being cut off and alone seems to be experienced by almost everyone. It is as much a part of depression as the feeling of extreme sadness.

As it is a symptom of our "illness," we may come to see that aloneness is not quite as clear-cut and terrible as we sometimes perceive it to be.

Our being alone has as much to do with our cutting ourselves off from others as it has with others cutting themselves off from us. People are there, but we feel we do not deserve their friendship, or that we are boring people, or that they might reject us if we ask them for some companionship, or . . . Most of us have our own (often hardly understood) reasons for keeping ourselves to ourselves. We may think we are doing the opposite of cutting ourselves off from people.

Ways out of the loneliness

If we have very few friends and relatives, to have any effect on a state of loneliness we need to make two basic changes:

- Change how we think about people so that we really believe (as opposed to just thinking we believe) that we want to meet more people.
- Actually get out and meet more people. This probably means changing our behavior.

Remember, though, that sometimes people really are unfriendly.

How we think about people

Lonely people often have some negative self-talk (see chapter 19) that goes something like this:

"Well, I couldn't be friends with that type of person anyway."
"If I make friends they will find out what I am like, and then they will reject me."
"No one would want to be my friend anyway."

We are not so much alone as experiencing the fear of what it would be like to be close to someone. Having friends and making relationships is a risky and painful business. We defend ourselves from it because we learned about how tough it was years ago.

Maybe we expect too much?

If we are unrealistic about what people are able to give us in terms of friendship and tender loving care, we will inevitably be disappointed.

A "good enough" friendship might be better than no friendship at all.

Activity

- Spend the next few weeks arguing with your negative thinking about loneliness.
- Get fit. Join a fitness club. You'll meet people, get healthier, look better, and be more the sort of person people want to spend time with.
- Join at least one other group or club. No one ever made more friends by watching television.
- Make a list of people you already know. Plan who you could meet during this week.
- Make a list of the things that you like doing on your own. Feeling good about being alone is part of the battle against loneliness.
- There are groups that exist for those who are lonely. Join a self-help group. Ask someone who runs such a group for some addresses. See the resources list at the back of the book.
- Go out now and talk to either a neighbor or someone at a local shop. If you can't do that, write a letter or phone someone.

If all your efforts come to nothing, it may not be you that is the problem, but it may be others.

34

Reaching the overhang
and facing the impossible

The main thing in life is not to be afraid to be human.
—*Pablo Casals*

The news on television today is again too painful to watch. Wars, bitter and deadly, go on. In Africa, soldiers confiscate food that aid workers are trying to get to starving children. The television film shows tiny bodies being buried in shallow graves in the sand. Other children stand around, too weak to bother to brush the flies from their faces. A mother weeps, holding her starving baby to her empty breast.

My own child is confused by the death of one of her favorite teachers. How can I start to explain why someone so delightful and talented should die? What could I say to my children when their friend died in a car crash?

How do we take them from the protection of childhood when we soothe them by saying "It's okay," to the reality of life where it quite clearly isn't okay, at least not all the time and with no certainty that it will remain okay for very long?

We cannot explain our strange world, but no one could doubt the fact that it is cruel. Pain and sadness seem to come to everyone without any regard for how "good" they are or whether they "deserve" to face such suffering.

Job, a character in the Bible, had problems like this. He was a good man, but terrible things kept happening to him. His "comforters" tell him it's because he's a bad person. That goes down like a lead balloon, and Job tells them exactly what he thinks of them!

Miserable comforters are you all! Will your long-winded speeches never end?
—*Job, during his depression*

Once when I was watching a religious television channel, some preacher said that if we worshipped God and worked hard we would become rich and happy. This is one of the most ridiculous things I have ever heard. It could become a justification for letting the poor and homeless stay poor and homeless because they didn't work "hard enough."

Bad things happen to good people

Any observation of human life soon reveals that awful things don't just happen to bad people. There are happy rich criminals, and sad and poor honest people. Bad things happen to good people. Why God allows it I have no idea.

Saying that God has it all under control or that he moves in mysterious ways is no answer. It may be true, but it's like people telling us we will be "glad" we have been depressed. Really?

Maybe there just isn't an answer

Maybe life is such an anomaly that to try to find answers of any sort is doomed to failure. Maybe we will not get total freedom from our depression but develop an ability to handle life sufficiently well despite it. As time goes on, we get better at recognizing the truths about the pain of being alive.

The closest I ever arrive to finding some sort of satisfactory explanation of life and depression for myself is when I realize that we just cannot know the answers. Life has elements so inexplicable and so utterly awful that we simply cannot see what they are really about. It's like the smocking on a dress that I made for my beautiful goddaughter. The finished product, the stitches on the front, looked pretty, but if I looked at it from the reverse side as I was doing it, it was an incredible tangled mess of thread and knots.

Maybe in this life on earth we are always looking at things from this limited perspective: the wrong side. It looks like a chaotic mess with no pattern or sense to it. But when we reach the afterlife, we shall be looking at it all from the other side, and we will see the reasons, the pattern, the sense in it all. Maybe!

Facing the impossible

Most people come up against impossible parts of life at some stage. Some days we can barely cope with the overhangs, those impossible sections where we have to get over a huge lump of rock that juts out so far we need to go upside down for a bit. Other days we are more able to deal with them. Or we find another route.

Some days we look at what we need to face in life, and it seems too difficult to face. Ever.

"Love her? After what happened?"

"Forgive him? After what he did to me?"

"Learn to accept myself? You must be joking!"

"Believe that this depression will end? Give me one shred of evidence that that is true!"

Getting over the impossible stretches

- Work with someone on it. Join a self-help group. Ask your doctor for help or find a therapist. Never attempt an overhang without someone holding on very firmly to the lifeline.
- Find a different route. There is usually more than one way of doing something.
- Don't make major decisions when the going is tough.
- If you can, choose the easiest option! Depression is quite bad enough without making things any more difficult than they already are.

There's no such thing as a peace of soul approach to religion. It makes of God a gigantic Bayer aspirin . . . take God three times a day and you won't feel any pain.
—John Powell

35

"You'll be glad this happened"

In addition to trust in God, there will also emerge a trust in ourselves, a genuine belief in our own worth based not on endeavours but on the gift of being cherished. . . . We are acceptable to God because he is loving and merciful and not because we have done good things.
—*Myra Chave-Jones,* Listening to Your Feelings

Irritating people who tell you that in the end you will be glad that all this hell of depression happened just do not know what it is really like, or have forgotten. No one could ever be glad that it happened. But what does seem to be true is that having the low times helps you to appreciate the highs.

I'm not an authority on standing at the top of the cliff and feeling great. But I can see that in comparison with the bottom of the abyss, it is rather good. Maybe if life were that good all the time we would become rather like bratty children who are so used to getting their own way that they become intolerable.

Perhaps the experience of being depressed makes us into "better" people. By that I mean people who are sensitive to and caring about the needs of others and who have experienced enough about life to begin to develop some understanding of what makes people so varied and interesting.

We acquire a growing appreciation of the extent of human suffering. In my own very narrow experience of life, I think I notice that those people who have suffered are those who are broad enough to open their arms to comfort those who are in pain.

One of the few good things about depression is that, like all pain, it is saying something.
—*Myra Chave-Jones*

I suppose that in climbing, if it were really easy to get up every climb, there would be little point in doing so, and we would not have the unique feeling of success when we got to the top. The harder the climb, the better it feels. Maybe in some way we are made into more complete human beings if our climb through life is tough.

I don't know. That could begin to sound horribly trite. All I know is that although the people who tell me I will be glad this happened are quite wrong, often at the end of a really difficult climb I will stand at the top, utterly exhausted but reveling in a feeling that I experience at no other time. It is as if I will never feel anything is difficult in the rest of my life. If I can do that, I can do anything.

Now that I have faced depression and recovered (even though at times I slither back down into it), how can anything in life ever seem as difficult as that?

Even if I think of the very worst thing that could ever happen to me—the death of my partner or one of my children—could that really be any worse than that clammy, silent hell? Of course it might be, how can I know? But having endured and overcome depression, I think that I have some of the resources to face the very worst that life might throw at me. I think.

Maybe it is those skills that I learned so painfully throughout those periods of depression that will be the same skills that I will need to survive the next thirty years. Facing depression is one of the hardest parts of human existence. If we can do that, we can do anything!

Tips for dealing with the "Pull up your socks" brigade

There are enormous numbers of people out there who belong to what I call the "Pull up your socks" brigade. Most of them are impossible to miss as they tend to be fairly vocal, but others are more difficult to spot. They can be friendly and sympathetic at first, then when you least expect it, they launch off into telling you to "pull yourself together." (If only it were that easy.)

Here are some tips to help deal with them.

Beware of whom you trust.

You won't get anywhere without trusting someone, but be very cautious. People need to prove themselves to be trustworthy. (You wouldn't attempt a climb with ropes you didn't know were trustworthy.)

The "I'm far worse off than you" people are extraordinarily difficult to deal with.

The really important things to tell yourself are that they have desperate needs too, but depression is never, ever about a competition to see which person is the worst off; we could easily become one of these people! Beware!

Beware of those who say they have never been depressed.

They deliver this statement complete with a cryptic paragraph about how there have been many events in their life that could have led to depression. This really is no more than a complex way of saying that they are worse off than you are and that because they did not get depressed, you shouldn't either, so pull yourself together.

These people are to your recovery and well-being what a major avalanche is to climbing. You need to avoid them or shut down your emotions and placate them, then make a swift exit.

Try the following:

• Walk away. The best way to do this is to suddenly remember that you have an appointment (with your journal) or to say, "Well I really must get going," "I'm glad we ran into each other," "How nice to see you." Whatever you do, keep talking. That is absolutely vital. Any drivel will do, but you must keep it up until you are out of earshot.
• If you can't get away, smile benignly and shut down your emotions at the same time. Developing this mask is a basic survival skill for facing depression.
• Develop a noncommittal *Hmm.* You need to practice this in your bedroom until you get it right. It should say neither yes nor no. People will usually take it to mean what they want it to mean. So, they tell you to pull yourself together. You smile and go *Hmm.* They think you mean "Well, how kind of you, I never thought of trying to pull myself together. I really will try harder. Silly me. You are a darling to be so kind and helpful." But what you actually

mean is "You insensitive idiot. I could tear you limb from limb. You'd better evaporate right now or you're history."

- Suggest you have a cup of tea or coffee or a Coke. Babble.
- If babbling fails or you just haven't got the strength to do it, deflect them into talking about themselves. Deflection is easy with the "I've had lots of reasons in my life to be depressed, but I didn't let it get to me" types because, like most people, they like to talk about themselves. If that fails, resort to politics, sex, or religion.
- If you feel strong enough, being a bit assertive can do wonders. I'm not exactly suggesting that attack is a good defense, but assertiveness is a good thing to try to develop anyway. You can silence the most intrepid member of the pull-your-socks-up brigade by telling him or her that many of the world's truly great people were depressed, that it's all a part of the creative spirit and a sign of true genius (in our case yet to be recognized). You can also get someone going by asking how she or he would arrive at world peace in three easy stages. This can usually guarantee to deflect even the most intrepid person.

There are other well-meaning people who tell you that you will look back on all this in ten years' time and be glad of it. They may have trod the shadow of the valley of death themselves. Take great care. The best tack is to get them to tell you about it. Just like elderly and experienced climbers, you can learn a lot from listening to people like this, about what it was that made them depressed and how they climbed out of it. If they are helpful, write down why. Then use that as a basis for you to help someone else.

You may not feel you could ever help anyone. Life feels as if it will always be this bad. But it won't. One day someone will reach out to you for help. Helping others is the only way I was ever able to make sense of the hell of depression, because it is like dealing with bereavement: You have to experience it to have any idea of what it is like.

**Even though I walk through the valley of the shadow of death,
I will fear no evil, for you are with me.**
—*The Psalmist*

36

Missing the foothold

Why have you forgotten me, God?
—The Psalmist

The climb out of depression is neither smooth nor easy. Some days or weeks we feel good and know we are making progress. Then, sometimes for no clear reason, our grip on life loosens. Something we thought we could deal with suddenly overwhelms us. Our sleep patterns are disturbed again, including perhaps the dreadful early morning wakening that so many of us experience. We slip back into old eating habits. We slip back into old thinking habits. The nightmares return. Suddenly we feel unable to communicate with anyone.

This has been my experience during the last few weeks. I know it is depression beginning again. I have learned to recognize the early signs. It is not drastic or debilitating. Just a lingering fatigue and those telltale symptoms: bursting into tears at the slightest problem, waking early, already defeated, and finding that the things I have previously enjoyed are boring. Nothing is fun anymore. Yet I know it is not that bad . . . yet. What I want to try to do is to not let it get any worse. Can I do that?

Stopping it from getting any worse
First, try to establish that your hold on the cliff face is secure enough. It's not very secure, but it's secure enough. What I mean by that is that you have enough strength to face the next ten minutes. The thought of getting through the day is ghastly. The thought of facing next week (and the start of term) is so dreadful that I get panic attacks. But I have enough of a hold to be able to face the next ten minutes.

I've made a list of the things I *must* do today and those that I *could* do today. (I've tried to make it an attainable list.) It will make me feel good as I check things off. I probably won't get them all done, but everything marked off makes me feel good and strengthens my grip on the rock face. I'm holding on well enough. That's "good enough" for now.

Second, be very aware of what is happening. This gives me the feeling that I have control over my life. Simply being aware that it is happening is important. Learning to recognize our own early symptoms is a crucial skill to acquire. Mine may be very different from yours. Other symptoms that friends have told me about:

wanting to drink more (of the alcoholic kind)
extreme impatience
not being able to concentrate
a lack of interest in anything

It is a good idea to write down how you feel in your journal. This may give you insight into those early symptoms. We might be tempted to see ourselves as sitting alone at the foot of the cliff in total darkness bawling our eyes out. That may not be the true picture. It may be that we are hanging on. Just.

Being aware of hanging on

This awareness of ourselves will only come with practice. There are all sorts of circumstances that can influence us profoundly and tend to make us think that things are worse than they really are. I find these are often related to physical well-being. For example, I know that one aspect of my present sense of slithering down the cliff is the virus I recently suffered. Any illness, flu, or the mildest of tummy bugs, leaves me drained and depressed.

I am also aware that simply being physically tired makes me feel things are worse than they really are. Being unable to cope after a late night is pretty obvious.

It took me years to recognize that what I call "creeping tiredness" accumulates over months. Looking back on my child-rearing years this was probably at the root of a lot of the depression: simple tiredness. In my case, unrecognized simple tiredness. If you are like me, this general fatigue takes over life. I went around like a zombie. It is important to develop an awareness of what is happening to us. It's your body; you need to take control over what you do to it and what is done to it.

Okay, so it's today, and I know that I am low. I know why—well, some of the reasons why—and I don't want to sink any lower. What can I do about it?

How do I stop slithering down?

- Believe that I am still on the cliff face and not at the foot.
- Believe that things will get better! That's not easy, especially because in the process of getting better, most things get worse. It's like tidying things—the kitchen cupboards, our desk, or the room of a three-year-old: There is always a terrible, terrible phase to get through first.
- Take great care of myself. When my fingers are sore and I know that my grip on the rock face is not as good as it needs to be, drastic action is required. Don't waste time by thinking that everything will take care of itself. It won't. Firm and decisive action is needed. It is our self-survival that is at stake.
- Get plenty of rest. This is vital.
- Have a good diet and take vitamin supplements.
- Some exercise really helps. I feel invigorated, refreshed, and renewed. Even just a few stretching exercises in the bedroom can help.
- Time on my own. An extrovert might take care of herself by going out with friends or having some people come to her house. That fills me with horror! The principle is to do something that we *choose* to do without feeling guilty about it! Guilt, sitting around feeling sorry for ourselves, or expecting someone else to do something about our insecure grip on the cliff will only make it worse. There is no need to feel guilty about taking a break and doing what we want to do in order to get over some crisis. It's okay to have crises. It's human to have crises, and it's okay to be human.
- Use the negative-thoughts chart in chapter 19.
- Although I prefer to write, it is also important to talk to someone. There is a big difference between expecting someone else to do something about it all (in the sense of handing over responsibility) and the very sensible act of sharing our feelings with someone.

Recognizing the progress

Everyone has bad phases. Provided we can see that we are more or less safe on our section of the cliff, by stopping for a bit and planning our next move very carefully, we will come to no harm.

Having a bad or a difficult phase is not the same as falling off:

- We're not at the foot again.
- We will learn something from this particular difficulty even if it is only that we have forgotten how absolutely dreadful it feels to have a bad phase.
- We have a valid reason for pampering ourselves a little. (Great! An excuse to have chocolate.)

Think

- Look back over the last few weeks or months and think about the progress you have made. There may not be much, but there is probably some.

Happiness is like coke—something you get as a by-product in the process of making something else.
—Aldous Huxley

More about **diet and exercise** in chapter 15.

37
Reaching the top

Happiness does not lie in happiness, but in the achievement of it.
—Fyodor Dostoyevsky

Everything ends. At least everything that is on earth and within our experience ends. (Well, I'm sure that the love that we give to others in our lifetime goes on and on inside those we have loved, so in a sense love never ends.) That is one thing that we can say is "good" about depression: It comes to an end. For some of us that end is only temporary. For others the end is after years of struggle during which we become different people. For most of us, this "end" is not a mountaintop of ecstasy. And it is certainly not the beginning of a wonderful life, joy, and eternal bliss! If we expect life to be like that we will certainly be disappointed.

But one day a moment comes when it seems that the burden has lifted. The climb seems easier today. We have an unexplainable feeling of lightness and joy inside our innermost being. We realize that the depression has lifted.

Yes, experience tells us that it may not stay lifted, but we are thrilled to get a bit of respite, and we learn to take a breather while we can. This is a time to remember to write in our journal. This is an experience we must record because the memory of it will be crucial to our future well-being. Should the climb become horrendous again (and it probably will), being able to read about the time when we felt great will be one way to cope. A way to survive. Evidence that life will not always be that bad.

There are two problems with feeling we have reached the top of the cliff. One is the "tiger in the cage" problem, and the other is the "optimist" problem.

The tiger in the cage
There are several versions of the story of the tiger in the cage. It is about becoming so used to life as a depressed person that we continue to behave as though we were depressed, when we aren't: "learned helplessness" some people call it.

The story goes that a tiger is shut up in a cage for years. She paces up and down trying to break free. She paces up and down for so long that when finally the cage is removed she continues to do just that. She doesn't see the significance of the removal of the bars and goes on pacing in the way she has learned, unable to appreciate the freedom that is hers.

We can be like that. Life is such a struggle that we learn to behave in certain ways. We expect life to be a drag. We expect to get exhausted. We expect to cry. We expect the days to be long and gray. We have learned to behave as depressed people. So when the depression lifts, we cannot recognize it. We don't make the best use of our freedom, and we go on behaving as if we were still trapped in the horrors of depression.

The optimist

The other side is that we can get so excited **when our** depression has gone that we fail to make allowance for the fact that it may come back. It's disastrous to think that because it has gone, it has gone for good. True, some people do recover from depression, and it seems not to recur, at least not with such intensity. But the realistic thing to do is to be thrilled at reaching the top of the cliff but be ready for the next part of the climb.

At no time is life one long party without troubles and cares. It's like climbing Helvellyn in the English Lake District. You just get to what you think is the top and then you see another summit some way off.

On several occasions I have made the mistake of letting myself think that my depression is over for good. I get so carried away with how fantastic it feels to be free of it that I forget to be realistic. Then when the old depressed feelings return, they come as a terrible shock.

The most useful thing I have been taught about the good times is to use them as preparation for the bad times. Rather like the idea of putting out a safety net. Life does feel a bit like walking a tightrope. One slip and that's it: You're off. But if there is a safety net, we need not worry.

We may as well accept that we are going to fall off. So, while we are feeling okay, it is a good idea to prepare for those bad days. We need to make plans for what we will do when we fall off. The idea is to be able to:

- Recall the good times. This will help us to see that the depression will come to an end.
- Prepare strategies for dealing with the awfulness of depression.
- Learn more about ourselves. What is it that I like doing and that makes me feel good? What is it that makes me feel depressed?
- Learn to be kind to ourselves.

These things will help, so that when we do fall, it will only be a little loss of dignity, and we will be able to bounce safely on the cliff face. When we get our feet onto a ledge, we can prepare for the climb again.

Maybe it is better to imagine that the climb of life is one that goes on forever. Sometimes we get to the top of this cliff, and the way ahead is a mile of springy turf. But there is another cliff ahead.

For now though, the climb has ended. It is flat. The sun is shining, the puffins are flying in and out of their burrows, the sea pinks are beautiful, and the smell of the ocean is exhilarating. It feels like heaven.

We would be pessimists of the very worst kind if we let the thought of the climb ahead weigh us down so much that we lost the delights of today. Yes, we must keep it in our minds—life will not always be this good—but we must let ourselves enjoy the sheer excitement of the freedom that today, at least, is good.

Joy is the infallible sign of the presence of God.
—*Madeleine L'Engle*

Good days have become for me like the very end of the C. S. Lewis Narnia stories. At the end of *The Last Battle*, when the world of Narnia comes to an end and the high king, Peter, pulls shut the door on the dead world, the children follow Aslan and the animals into a world that is bigger, brighter, and better than Narnia. Yet it too is Narnia. It is all that they have loved and more. Aslan urges them, "Further up and further in!" and the dogs, the children, and the unicorn run farther into their new heaven, each part getting better than the one before.

That's how it seems on the good days, and we try to go farther and farther in. But there still may be huge cliffs ahead of us. Life, it would seem, is always a journey.

My greatest asset is that I am constantly changing.
—*Jane Fonda*

The choice

Ultimately I have a choice. I can go on fighting reality and insisting that life "should" be wonderful, carefree, happy, and so on. I can adopt the sort of world-owes-me-a-living attitude that some depressed people (and others) demonstrate.

Or I can get down to the nitty-gritty of it all and choose to take as my baseline that "life is difficult." This difficulty lies in the complexities of ourselves and our lifetime struggle to understand our inner selves. It is the unpredictable and apparently totally unfair way that life (and death) goes on. Tomorrow my world may be shattered by the death of my child. If that were to happen, I know that I would just want to die too. I cannot know what is out there; that is how life is.

Given the uncertainties and complexities of life, maybe it is surprising that there is as much happiness in the world as there is.

Happiness is like a sunbeam, which the least shadow intercepts.
—*Chinese proverb*

38

Now for the mountain!

Nothing is so beautiful as spring.
—*Gerard Manley Hopkins*

The sheer joy of living is, inexplicably, here today, and to feel it is great! The last bout of depression—six months of struggle, anxiety, fear, and almost daily tearfulness—has at long last ended. I realize that this break may not last long. Today I intend to enjoy it.

I've been walking in my garden. The snowdrops are exquisite. The crocuses spring out of the lawn in daring yellow, and the robins are building their nest in the apple tree. I wanted to drink up the dew and soak in the morning sunshine. It seemed I had never seen such colors or smelled such freshness. It all felt new, different, alive.

The joy and pleasure that I feel today may be great because they are in such stark contrast to how I've been feeling for the last few months. The winter has been long and dreary. Some days were so bleak that it seemed as if life could never be any different. But maybe nature needs its winter, its time of rest and re-creating.

Although I could never be "glad" about depression, today I know that I recognize the joy and freedom because I've had so much of the trapped feeling. The pain that I've felt helps me to recognize the happiness. As one of my climbing friends said to me, "If we didn't have our lows we would never appreciate our highs."

It's when it is all over that we can look back down the cliff and recognize the help that we have had.

Maybe the view that we will be "glad" that it happened comes from the understanding that there is something about suffering that helps a person to grow emotionally, to learn to understand herself better, and consequently to understand others better.

Rethinking our lives

The growth toward accepting and understanding our depressed feelings, and seeing them in balance with all the other features of our lives, is a very personal journey.

As the spring comes we start to see new ways to move forward in life. The death and the bleakness are not the end. The seeds that we planted last autumn are dead, but in their place are new green shoots. That seems to be the way that our world operates. For new life there has to be death. There has to be some stage of resting, of rethinking and replanning.

He who can traverse the pit of darkness will emerge a stronger, more compassionate person.
—*Martin Israel*

For me, periods of depression have been opportunities to reappraise my life. Of course, I could not see it at the time. But looking back I can see how they were phases during which I was able to think about what I really wanted in my life.

I have come to see the depression as the start of seeing the reality. The world *is* a crazy and ambiguous place, and a part of our journey is recognizing that and somehow learning to live with it.

When all is going well we do tend to take things for granted. When things are going badly, we become more balanced. We see what is really important in life. Money and possessions, career, status, and other things society tries to tell us are of supreme importance come to mean less than the little things we can miss in our busyness. We come to appreciate the little things, like the smile of a child, or the sound of the birds at dawn, or the joy at seeing the first flowers of spring.

Thou hast made us for thyself, and our soul is restless till it rests in thee.
—*Augustine of Hippo*

There *will* be an end to our depression. We begin to see that end as we learn to see that we are worthy people, that we *are* loved, even though it may not feel as if we are.

When you really want love, you will find it waiting for you.
—*Oscar Wilde*

Depression can mean that life is much better than it was before. It is more honest. More reality based. More about the things that really matter.

When we get to the top of the cliff in rock climbing, the harder our struggle has been the greater our sense of achievement, relief, and, at times, ecstasy. At last we can lie down, rest our aching arms, and just let the sun beat down on us.

We lie there, maybe a little amazed at what we have accomplished. If we look with honesty at our lives and what we have been through, maybe we need to give ourselves some credit for sticking at it and surviving this far! To get even part of the way through a depressive phase takes extraordinary courage. To get to the end of it is perhaps the greatest achievement of our lives.

It is good to look back at it all and take time to remember what it was like at the foot of the cliff. Incredibly we find sometimes that we can hardly remember the very worst parts. It is as if they were so terrible that they have been blotted out of our memories—a kind of defense mechanism that we develop. It's rather like the way we forget the pain of childbirth as we take the tiny little person into our arms for the first time. The immensity of the joy blots out the pain.

Going on

It is so important in the good times to go on, not to go back and recriminate. Most of us have horror stories about the ways that we were treated during our depression. Somehow we have to let these go; otherwise we will be constantly moaning about how hard the struggle to get up was, instead of enjoying the sunshine and the rest at the top.

We don't know what lies ahead, but we must keep moving on.

I said to the man who stood at the gate of the year, "Give me a light that I may tread safely into the unknown," and he replied, "Go out into the darkness and put your hand into the hand of God. That shall be to you better than light and safer than a known way."
—*From* God Knows *by Minnie Louise Haskins, quoted by King George VI in his Christmas 1939 broadcast, during the first few months of the Second World War*

I had this quote about going out into the unknown in my mind from the very start of writing this book. Writing felt like going out into the unknown. It is obvious that to some extent I feel vulnerable writing about my experiences of depression. During the two years it has taken to write it I have had some very deep depressive episodes. It was excruciating to be writing about such terrifying fear.

Yet it has also been a joy to write it. I believe that our lives are made richer by sharing our feelings and thoughts, painful though this sharing may be. It is only when we reach out and take a risk that we can connect with others. It is then that the love, peace, and new life at the top of the cliff become possible.

Sharing is one of the key features of the climb. We come to see that being human is about being a part of a "community." It is about relating to others. The annihilating aloneness of depression begins to heal as we allow others to draw close.

When I come out of a depressed phase I read the words of the Revelation to John at the end of the Bible. They make me cry because they remind me of the funerals of people I have loved. They remind me of death, but also of new beginnings. John says that God will wipe away every tear from our eyes and that there will be no more mourning or crying or pain, because God himself will be making everything new.

In the beautiful picture, God is sitting on his throne surrounded by a jeweled landscape that we, as his children, will inherit. The crystal water of the river of life comes from the throne, and when we drink from this water, we will never be thirsty or want for anything again.

Whatever the images used, this tells me that I am loved and that there will be an end to the struggles and the darkness one day.

I am loved, therefore I am.

Don't look down

We learn not to look down when we climb. We don't need to see where we have been. It's terrifying anyway. We only need to remember to learn from it.

We must go on. The summit is our only goal. The handholds above us look completely inadequate, but other people have found them, so we must have faith that they will be okay for us too. We need:

- to think ourselves into life at the top.
- to learn to trust more in the lifeline and those holding it.
- to have hope. Others, who felt as bad as we do, did finally make it. We can too.
- to go on practicing the new skills we learned during depression: being kind to ourselves and being in touch with what we are thinking and feeling.
- to keep on working at self-understanding and at building up our self-esteem.
- to learn to "let go." Hanging on to old hates and bitterness is one very effective way of slithering down again.
- to learn to accept that fluctuating moods are "normal," that it's "normal" to have to go back a few stages before we can go on.
- to learn to keep on climbing. Life is tough, but the more we keep plodding on with the journey the better we get at dealing with it.

Depression can be a new beginning. There *is* life after depression!

39
On reflection

In this final chapter I've pulled together some of the most important things that I have learned over the past few years.

Making time to nurture ourselves
Making time for ourselves is crucial, not introspective, not selfish!

• Put it in your diary!

New starts
As I struggle to control my eating, I feel I have learned something crucial to the climb out of depression. If we are desperate to have a good day of healthy eating, and by nine o'clock in the morning we've eaten not just our breakfast of healthy fruit and cereal but also six pancakes, three chocolate bars, and a box of cookies, we must learn not to go into all-or-nothing thinking: "I've totally blown my healthy eating forever, so I might as well have another pancake and give up being healthy. I'm just hopeless." We need to learn that we can have a totally new start at any time of day or night, and that new start begins right now.

• This is one of the Great Truths of life: A new start can happen anywhere and at any time.

We are special

Although the world is full of suffering, it is full also of the overcoming of it.
—*Helen Keller*

It is as we overcome our difficulties in life that we find within ourselves strengths and qualities that we did not know we had. We find within ourselves a very special kind of treasure: ourselves.

- Having learned (more or less) to turn around our negative thinking, we see our uniqueness, our value, and our special place in the world. (You might not be feeling "there" yet, but if you carry on climbing, you will get there.)

The wounded healer

Having been wounded, as we struggle to recover, we find we can help others also.

- We are "wounded healers," and that is a very powerful gift to share.

Do something!

It is clear that in order to get up the cliff, we must *do something*. I know there are days when we just can't. On those days or weeks it is important to rest. But that rest must be *for the purpose of preparing to do something* such as getting up. If we lie in bed too long, we are likely to spiral down into the depths again. None of us wants that; it is a hideous place to be.

So we must *do something!* This prevents the vicious cycle: We feel terrible so we lie down, but that makes us feel useless and worthless so we spiral down further.

We must get out of the habit of seeing ourselves as being depressed forever, as never being able to get better. Rather bizarrely, some people sometimes almost seem to relish the depressed state (perhaps because they want to remain the center of attention at home?).

Don't let that happen to you! *Do something*, even if it is only opening your eyes to look at the time or bringing into your mind the picture of a fresh, hot cup of coffee.

- We must commit to pushing ourselves when we can, yet acknowledge that there will be times when we can't.

Overcoming fear and anxiety

Part of our negative thinking are those "old tapes" from long ago that keep shouting to us in our mind and seem to be at the root of much of our anxiety. I've found cognitive and psychodynamic therapy really valuable in helping me to become more rational and to start to challenge the basis of my anxiety.

Last week, when my heart was pounding after something a relative did, I did the deathbed test. Will I worry about this on my deathbed? No! Then I'm not going to let it spoil my day now!

- We can make a plan of the things we will try to do over the next few months to reduce our anxiety: perhaps relaxation classes, making sure we take enough time off just to be ourselves and give ourselves time for family, hobbies, and so on. But it's not going to happen unless we make the commitment to *do something!*

Making a commitment to challenge ourselves

Depressed people talk about the challenges we face, and this is a healthy sign. Meeting up last week at a conference with some Depression Alliance members I haven't seen for several years, it was interesting to see so many people getting on with their lives, enjoying the challenges of things like running a self-help group, and so on.

Some people, sadly, seem to stay right where they are, and there must be many reasons for this. But I'd like to suggest that they stay in their depressed and anxious states so long because they are not challenging themselves sufficiently.

- It is crucial that we learn to challenge our negative thinking and deliberately set about changing that thinking. (This is what cognitive therapy is all about.)

The commitment to change

Close friends suffering from depression who have taken up challenges are committing themselves to change. We talk about making small changes, not huge ones that would overwhelm us.

We know we are changing. A dear friend who came to visit me a few weeks ago remarked on how very different I was from when we last met a couple of years ago. Yes. I know I am changing.

I'm often asked how we can set about changing. The activities within this book are starting points for change. In the diagram opposite I've outlined something I work on with groups of depressed people. It is a concept map of how we might change that you could work on by yourself or with a caregiver. You might take several days or even weeks to make a decision about what might be the best way to get you a bit farther up the cliff. There are no right answers. Your diagram might look very different from my example.

• It is crucial that we remember that we can all change. That is another Great Truth about life: We need to decide deliberately to change.

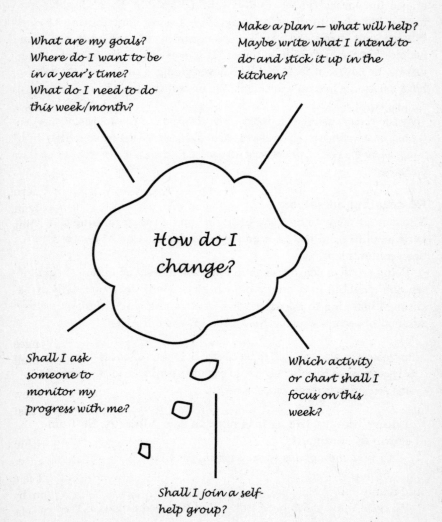

What are my goals?
Where do I want to be in a year's time?
What do I need to do this week/month?

Make a plan — what will help?
Maybe write what I intend to do and stick it up in the kitchen?

How do I change?

Shall I ask someone to monitor my progress with me?

Which activity or chart shall I focus on this week?

Shall I join a self-help group?

The commitment to learn contentment

"Life isn't fair!" some depressed people almost shout at me. That's right! Life isn't fair. But we don't improve our lives by moaning about it. Yes, things do go wrong. Yes, our plans don't always work out the way we hope. Yes, we were badly treated as children. Yes, it is terrible to be a victim of any kind of abuse. But we all get only this one chance of life on earth. Do we really want to spoil it by endlessly and impossibly wanting it to be different? Are we contributing to our future mental health by wanting revenge or by demanding things from people that we are unlikely to get? It is perfectly reasonable to want justice. Of course it is. But if it is never going to come, we will have a hard decision: Give up wanting it? Go on waiting for it?

- We can commit ourselves to finding peace of mind and contentment in the situation in which we find ourselves. From there we can set out to change our life for the better, making sure we choose to change things that can be changed!

Re-creating ourselves

The commitment to be more creative can be the very thing that will turn our life from the pain and gloomy destruction of depression to deep contentment.

Being creative doesn't seem to me to be merely an option. I think if we don't dabble in a hobby or bring creativity into our daily lives through listening to music or whatever, we risk stagnation, or, worse, we tend to become destructive—often toward ourselves.

- Re-creation is taking time off to be ourselves, to use our brains more fully, to become more balanced people, to end the destruction, to give ourselves time and space to reflect on our lives.

I don't like my life as it is now. In fact I hate it. So I am going to change it.
—*A young man at one of my workshops*

And finally . . .

We need to play! We need to be silly! We need to laugh! We need to find some way to have fun! If you feel a million miles away from that now, you won't always feel like that. You won't always feel this bad. There will come a day when you feel better.

Deep peace of the Running Wave to you.
Deep peace of the Flowing Air to you.
Deep peace of the Quiet Earth to you.
Deep peace of the Shining Stars to you.
Deep peace of the Son of Peace to you.
—*Old Celtic blessing*

Resources

There are a number of organizations that support depressed people in different ways. If this list doesn't include what you need, either search the web for "mental health" or contact one of the following organizations and ask for advice.

While the Internet is very helpful for finding information about climbing out of depression, **never buy any medication on the web.** It may be counterfeit or even poisonous; always obtain medication from a doctor.

Depression and Bipolar Support Alliance (DBSA)

This U.S.-based charity has an extremely informative website, including confidential screening for depression and advice on helping a loved one through depression or helping children who are depressed. You can also download free information on a huge range of topics, and they also publish newsletters, hold conferences, and facilitate many local self-help groups that enable depressed people to get in touch with others to share stories and provide mutual support. Their website is also in Spanish. There is also an **In Crisis** helpline available in the United States.

Information Helpline: 1-800-273-TALK
DBSA, 730 N. Franklin Street, Suite 501, Chicago, Illinois,
60654–7225
www.dbsalliance.org

Depression Alliance

This UK-based friendly and helpful organization runs self-help groups across the UK as well as an online group. They also offer support for caregivers and have an informative website that offers guidance for everything from surviving depression to taking medication. Their magazine, *A Single Step,* gives members an opportunity to express themselves and also provides more information for depressed people and their caregivers, including book reviews, and so on.

Information Helpline: 0845 123 2320
Unit 212 Spitfire Studios, 63–71 Collier Street, London N1 9BE,
England
www.depressionalliance.org

Centre for Addiction and Mental Health

Based in Canada, this organization has a website that provides useful information on the specific issues of addiction, along with a wide range of resources and recent research on depression and other mental health issues.
www.camh.net

American Mental Health Alliance

This organization will help you locate a therapist near you in the United States.
www.americanmentalhealth.com

National Institute of Mental Health

This U.S. government site provides information on the research and treatment of mental illness. Also available in Spanish.
www.nimh.nih.gov

MIND (National Association for Mental Health)

This UK charity provides support for those with mental health problems and campaigns for better mental health care.
www.mind.org.uk

SAD Association

Those who feel more depressed in the winter can contact this group for help. Using a light box when there is little or no sunshine can lift depression, and SAD can help you choose the best box.
P.O. Box 989, Steyning BN44 3HG, England
www.sada.org.uk

Samaritans

A twenty-four-hour helpline in the UK and some other countries.
Helpline: 08457 909090
www.samaritans.org.uk

Further reading

Sue Atkinson, *Breaking the Chains of Abuse* (London: Lion Hudson, 2006).

Sue Atkinson, *Building Self-Esteem* (London: Lion Hudson, 2001).

Barbara Baker, *When Someone You Love Has Depression* (London: Sheldon Press, 2003).

Eric Berne, *Games People Play* (New York: Grove Press, 1964).

Lucia Capacchione, *Recovery of Your Inner Child* (New York: Simon & Schuster, 1991).

Virginia Edwards, *Depression and Bipolar Disorders: Everything You Need to Know* (Toronto: Key Porter, 2002).

Mitch Golant and Susan K. Golant, *What to Do When Someone You Love Is Depressed* (New York: Henry Holt, 2007).

Thomas A. Harris, *I'm OK—You're OK* (New York: Harper Paperbacks, 2004).

Susan Jeffers, *Feel the Fear and Do It Anyway* (New York: Ballantine Books, 1987).

M. Scott Peck, *The Road Less Traveled* (New York: Simon & Schuster, 1978).

Dorothy Rowe, *Depression: The Way Out of Your Prison*, third edition. (London: Brunner-Routledge, 2003).

Dorothy Rowe, *Understanding Depression and Finding Freedom*, audio book (Thorsons Audio).

Lewis Smedes, *Forgive and Forget: Healing the Hurts We Don't Deserve* (New York: HarperCollins, 1996).

Lewis Smedes, *Shame and Grace* (New York: HarperCollins and Zondervan, 1993).

Charles L. Whitfield, *Boundaries and Relationships* (Deerfield Beach, FL: Health Communications, 1993).

Help with Meditation

Sue Atkinson, *Pathways Through Depression* (London: Lion Hudson, 2004).

Sue and David Atkinson, *In Times of Need* (London: Lion Hudson, 2008).

Gerard W. Hughes, *God of Surprises,* third edition (London: Darton, Longman and Todd, 2008).

John Powell, *Why Am I Afraid to Love? Overcoming Rejection and Indifference* (Thomas More, 1972).